2

MUCH

2

YOUNG

Trafford
PUBLISHING

Order this book online at www.trafford.com/08-0184
or email orders@trafford.com

Most Trafford titles are also available at major online book retailers.

Note for Librarians: A cataloguing record for this book is available from Library
and Archives Canada at www.collectionscanada.ca/amicus/index-e.html

ISBN: 978-1-4251-8476-6

*We at Trafford believe that it is the responsibility of us all, as both individuals
and corporations, to make choices that are environmentally and socially sound.
You, in turn, are supporting this responsible conduct each time you purchase a
Trafford book, or make use of our publishing services. To find out how you are
helping, please visit www.trafford.com/responsiblepublishing.html*

*Our mission is to efficiently provide the world's finest, most comprehensive
book publishing service, enabling every author to experience success.
To find out how to publish your book, your way, and have it available
worldwide, visit us online at www.trafford.com/10510*

Trafford
PUBLISHING™   www.trafford.com

North America & international
toll-free: 1 888 232 4444 (USA & Canada)
phone: 250 383 6864 ♦ fax: 250 383 6804 ♦ email: info@trafford.com

The United Kingdom & Europe
phone: +44 (0)1865 722 113 ♦ local rate: 0845 230 9601
facsimile: +44 (0)1865 722 868 ♦ email: info.uk@trafford.com

10 9 8 7 6 5 4 3 2

SIMPLICITY

&

ACHIEVEMENT

Through the years we have our insecurities, our worries and doubt

Wonder what the path life is taking and what it's all about

Sometimes we fail to take the step back and see what we have achieved to date

By taking the paths of uncertainty and walking through each and every gate

We wrap our emotions into tight parcels dressed for the entire world to see

When all we should do is embrace our world with a little simplicity

DEDICATION

Dedicated to Kim, Charlotte, Rose and George.

You are my now and my future ... my love to you always.

CONTENTS

PREFACE
WELCOME

WELCOME TO MY first book. It has taken me over 2 years to write and bring this book into publication. The length of time has been mainly due to the book being written by my own hand and as many of you will know, trying to find the time to actually sit down and write anything when you have work, family and social commitments can be a nightmare.

This book is about my life to date and how the things that I have experienced have not only shaped my world but also has moulded the way I apply myself to my working life. You will find within these pages my personal thoughts about many things including personal and business observations, but my original intention was to write something for my children to read one day so that they might see another side to me and understand a little better who I really am.

You will probably be able to critique my grammar and spelling throughout this book and this is fine with me and I want to leave things as they are, but you have to consider that these 'errors' stem from my lack of academic abilities in early life, remember I am just a normal guy, with faults and failings.

I am not going to tell you hear how to be a successful IT director, chief information officer (CIO) or business leader. I tell you this in advance for the following reasons:

+ I do not want you to think that I have that 'magic bullet' that will enable you to achieve your ambitions, and

+ I do not consider myself to be an expert in the field of motivational writing and psychology.

I will however be providing some hints, tips, insights and observations throughout the text that might help you, but this is not the main intention of this book.

As they say 'in every person is one book' and this happens to be mine and hope it may potentially help you understand my motivation and lead to your own successes.

Now let me introduce myself. My name is Philip Andrew Young or just Phil as I prefer to be called. I currently work as an interim IT director/chief information officer and whatever other work I feel I am capable of carrying out at the moment.

Just over 2 years ago I was awarded the 'CIO Innovator of the year' title at the UK Technology Innovation and Growth awards. Sounds very grandiose I know, but I am just a run of the mill family man who wants to get his thoughts down on paper and explore inside himself a little and maybe make you, the reader, think a little.

This is not an epic of a book, mainly due to the fact that I am forty-two years of age and do not have any sort of celebrity status or large amounts of money that would allow me to have a co-author / ghost writer who would embellish on my story and therefore make the chapters stretch. What you will read here is indeed very raw and personal, maybe too personal at times for my own comfort.

I would not be an innovator if I published a book in the usual way, so I have decided to do this with the resources that can be found on the internet and in networking groups. This I hope will help to keep the cost down and actually bring it into print, as I am sure it would not have made it otherwise.

Please now kick back and enjoy my world and thoughts and I would love to hear any comments that you might have.

Kind regards, Phil.

2 MUCH 2 YOUNG

FOREWORD

I DECIDED IT WAS time I wrote a book. A great idea I thought until the little gremlins in my head that have held me back on so many occasions throughout my life, started interjecting with comments such as, 'who will be interested in *your* book?', 'What makes *you* think it will be interesting to readers?', etc. So I sat on the idea for a number of months and then put a simple 'post' on www.ecademy.com. For those of you who do not know what www.ecademy.com is, it is a virtual space created on the internet for mainly professional people to exchange ideas and 'network'.

Anyway, I put the post on asking if people thought that a book about a CIO's life might be a good idea. The response was quite positive. Although, I did change the original title from 'Bollocks and the Bullshit' after someone suggested it may not be a good representation of what I am all about, ☺ spoil sport!

So, here we go. I hope you as the reader find this interesting, as you have probably invested time and money in buying it (if not, why not? I need to eat you know). Also, please feel free to use it as a doorstop or something useful if found not to be what you thought it might be, best to get some value out of it … lol (meaning 'laugh out loud', for those of you who are not of the 'MSN messenger' and 'text' age group).

Before I lead you down the twisty and sometimes bumpy road of my world, I would just like to take the opportunity to thank a few people who have made things happen for me and supported me. Firstly my family both close and extended. Dear reader, you will soon find out that I am not an easygoing person; I worry, I moan, I stress, but they never complain and I think they understand that this is what makes me who I am. Next, I would like to thank all the people who I have worked with in my professional life. Some of them might hate me, some might not, but again this is what makes me who I am.

Let's go …

CHAPTER 1
HERE I SIT

Let me explain, for those that don't know, what the term CIO means. It is an acronym for chief information officer – the Americanism for the term Information Technology director in the UK, you may need to know this to carry on reading. Now I can breathe a deep breath, put my head down and continue ...

It was a very heavy night last night, it is now 4.12 pm and I have been working in my office for a few hours, without much success. This is mainly due to a major lack of concentration and feeling more than a little rough, or should I say hungover. Last night saw the opening of a bar in our local town of Kidderminster, which my partner Kim had carried out the interior design work for. I went with the intention of having a look around to see her work, meet the owner and have a few drinks. Few drinks! I must remember not to drink double brandies in future!

So here I am sitting at my desk in my beautiful home. My desk is located on the gallery landing of our house and positioned between the various bedrooms. From one of these I can hear my stepson's Play Station buzzing away with him playing some game or other. If I could turn back time and try to imagine what my life would have been like in the future I could never have guessed this. It has been a roller coaster ride for me, comprising of lots of emotions, effort, sweat, turmoil and personal loss, but I would take a guess that so has yours. I have all the trappings of success; the nice home, car and holidays abroad, but it has not always been this way.

I have been trying to decide how best to take you through my personal and business life, should I start at the beginning or not? I think not; that would be so predictable and boring, so I will start at this current point in time and describe what my life is like at the moment and give you some idea of my family and things in general.

As I mentioned, I live near the town of Kidderminster located in Worcestershire, England. I hope it is politically correct for me to say England rather than the UK, as I do see myself as an Englishman, as many Scottish, Welsh and Irish people see themselves as native to their particular countries within the United Kingdom. However, some of my family, only going back three generations or so hail from further a field, my father's mother was Czech and my mother's grandfather's parents were Romani and her great grandmother was Austrian. But I am English and truly love my country.

My home is a timber-framed architect-designed house. It reminds me a little of the sort of house you see in North America, we even have a US mail box outside our front door; you know the ones with flags that you lift up to say 'you have mail'. Our flag is missing though, it seems our postman could not get the hang of it and ripped it off. Oh well, I will get my own back one day and process re-engineer his job away … lol (only joking!).

We did not have the house built; the previous owners did so eight years ago and I am extremely grateful to them as I feel I really belong here. Something I have rarely felt in my life to date.

The interior of the house is open plan and this means that you really need to be very okay about having noise around you all the time, something that I do find hard to accept when working, but love at other times. The house is busy nearly all of the time with children, friends of children, my partner, visitors and me usually shouting at one of the children to come and clean their bedroom. My home office is located on the gallery landing overlooking the lounge area and is great to work from and has good natural light, well great unless the children are home from school that is.

I have a fifteen-year-old daughter, Charlotte, from my previous marriage, a stepdaughter Rose, who is thirteen, a stepson George who is nine and an exceptional partner, Kim. Kim and I originally dated briefly when we were fifteen years old at high school and met up again just four years ago. I will go into more detail about this later in the book, but as you will get to learn, she is truly wonderful and always puts my world into perspective for me.

So, you have had a little bit of background information about me and now I want to jump back to February 2006.................

CHAPTER 2
I AM SO NERVOUS!

I AM SITTING HERE at a table in a room full of people at an awards ceremony at the Hilton Metropole hotel, London. Sitting at an awards ceremony, me? I have watched such things many times on television, but I never thought about what it might feel like to be attending one, and even more so actually being nominated for an award at one.

My heart is pounding hard; the truth is that it has been skipping beats for days now due to anxiety. I feel like it is not me sitting here, I am having some sort of out of body experience due to nervousness, a primeval protection thing that happens; 'the fight or flight response' I think it is called.

It is quite noisy and people are seated and talking all around me. I have guests at my table who are talking to me, but as I look at them it seems as though their mouths are opening and closing but no words are coming out, resembling a silent movie. 'Can someone turn on the subtitles please?', I cannot comprehend anything at the moment; I nod my head politely as they speak and hope I do not offend them by nodding at the wrong things or laughing when no joke has been told.

The truth is that in real life (not to be confused with my work-ing life) I am a very nervous and shy person and always have been. I have had to push myself hard and put on performances all my life that make me seem more confident than I actually am. I consider my whole working life to have been one giant performance, trying to impress and prove that I am a 'sound bet' at what I do. It is very hard to combat the inferiority complex one can get when one comes from a working class background such as mine.

I am sitting here wondering if I could possibly have won the award for 'CIO Innovator of the year'; this constant nagging in my head has sent me into a downward spiral of emotions; emotions I thought I had learnt how to conquer and overcome whilst going along life's journey, but obviously I have not. I am forty-one years old, and at this present time I feel like a child, a child who is looking around for the support of its mother and father. They are not here of course; even if I could have invited them I would hate for them to see me about to *fail*. Instead, I am here with people from many different companies who rep-resent some of the cream of British industry and 'I do not stand a chance of winning this award!' I keep saying this over and over in my head, to prepare myself for the inevitable failure and to enable me to shake off the disappointment that I know I will feel. I am trying to calm myself down, breathing deeply; I know I will pass out if I don't.

We are in the grand banqueting suite of the hotel; the room is full, with fifty circular tables, holding around ten people at each and the large ornate chandeliers have their lights dimmed to add further ambiance to the occasion. The majority of people have come wearing 'black tie' as it is an awards event, but I am not. 'Why have I done this?' you might well ask, 'why indeed?' I thought it would be nice to be a little different. Huge mistake, big mistake! To coin a phrase from Julia Roberts; all it makes me feel is that I am sticking out like a sore thumb and this is something that is causing me further anguish. As I said, I am a shy person and drawing attention to myself is not something I like to do. I am one of those people who tend to fly below life's radar, only raising their head occasionally when necessary or if totally unavoidable.

The presentation of the awards, the main event as it were, takes place after dinner has been served. I eat my meal, but I have no idea what I am eating really. It is not me sitting here, it's just a representation of me; the nerves are really getting to me. The tables are cleared and the lights are dimmed further, the guest speakers do their thing and I clap at the appropriate times, but I am not really listening, then the awards start ...

The CIO Innovator award is about the fifth to be presented. I keep my head tucked down and look at the card that is now in my hands. I tick off the winner of each award on the order of service as they are announced. Representatives from great and large brand companies are presented with awards and this only makes me more conscious of how prestigious the awards are and that I might as well go home right now.

My category is next. I do not stand a chance of winning. I once more try to control my nerves. The other nominees are from larger organisations than the one I represent and have a considerably higher profile than I; in some cases they have won several awards spanning a number of years. I go further into myself hoping to hide from any impending failure and practice in my head how to be dignified in defeat. Like anyone would, deep down, I really do hope that my name will be mentioned, but I also hope it's not, as I might not be able to stand up due to my shaking legs.

The nominees and company names for my category are read out with various tables of people clapping loudly as they are mentioned, my table included, and then what seems like a decade passes ...

I look down at the card in my hand and see my hands shaking; I am ready to tick off the winner's name and am continuing to prepare myself to clap them to the stage. The host compère starts his sentence, *'and the winner of the CIO Innovator of the year for a private sector organisation is* [long pause] ... [eternal pause] ... *Phil Young of Amtrak.'* I am in total shock and awe of the moment.

Fortunately, my 'acting mode' kicks my body into auto-pilot

and I stand and remove my jacket from the back of my chair, put it on and walk towards the stage from our table that is positioned over halfway back in the room. Music is playing loudly in the background and the compère is talking to the audience about my achievements, although I hear none of this as the sound of my pounding heart drowns it out. Its not me stood here! I feel as though I am shaking from head to toe as I walk; I hope this is not visible to anyone else. God, I'm so insecure.

I manage to get to the front of the room without making a complete fool of myself by falling over a table, accepting the award and shake hands with the presenter. Thank goodness I do not have to make an acceptance speech as I think I would have a heart attack on the spot.

This is now the professional me on show here, Phil Young, Head of IT, not the little boy I feel I still am at stressful times such as this.

2 MUCH 2 YOUNG

CHAPTER 3

ADRENALIN

I RETURN TO THE table, my guests are clapping me as I approach and champagne corks are popping. I soon start to remember that this is not only a great achievement for me, but also for the people around me, those people at the table who have contributed to the award by being exceptional suppliers to the company and myself. Also one of my direct reporting managers Joe Dudley, who has contributed a great deal to the projects that have led to this moment, is here with me and I am very happy that he is able to share in the occasion.

I come back to reality with a bump and I become that which I have neglected to be all evening, a host to my guests.

My company's PR executive is with us and is insistent that I move away from the table to various locations inside the room and also in the foyer to have my picture taken for our company's press releases. This again makes me uncomfortable, as people are looking at me. Stood here with my award held out in front of me and having my picture taken, all I can think of is that I must look like an arrogant so-and-so. I do not feel natural in the poses I am asked to hold. Kate Moss, I am not.

I eventually get a chance to run off to the men's room. All the nerves have made me desperate to pee and once out I take some time out to call home from my mobile phone. I am so excited on the phone and the adrenaline is still pumping through me. Kim answers and before she can say anything I more or less shout down the phone, 'I have won!' Although I had been playing down my chances of winning, she knew how much the award would mean to me and is thrilled when I tell her the outcome. I hear her tell the children who are hovering in the background and I can hear them jumping around the lounge, cheering.

This is one of the proudest moments of my life; not winning the award, but hearing those I love cheering for me; something that gives me a warm glow inside. I fill up with tears, wipe a few away and compose myself before returning to my guests in the banqueting room.

God, how I wish Kim was here with me to share this moment at first hand. I miss her and the children when I am away from them and these awards and emotions have just compounded my feelings.

The room is now clearing and it's about 11pm but I am not ready to sleep. Certain members of my party decide to retire, but I head for the bar area in the hotel with some of my guests. I need a drink and to relax and savour the moment.

We sit, talk and drink. I am so pumped up I cannot stop talking and I must be a little annoying to people. At 2.00am people make their excuses and leave and I head to my bedroom on the seventh floor, a nice double executive room that is warm and well decorated in a contemporary sort of way. I place my award on the top of the television cabinet and look at it. It is a perspex design, about the size of an A4 piece of paper, with the UK Technology and Growth award's logo seeming to float inside it and the inscription, 'CIO Innovator of the year'. Underneath this is written 'Phil Young, Amtrak'. I read it over and over as though to make me believe that it is real.

I undress and get into bed. Sleep is impossible, but I dim the lights and lie still with my eyes wide open peering at the award occasionally to make sure it's not all a dream and then I begin to reflect. I reflect not just on the evening but also on how I have got to this point in my life and career, a winner at last, but why do I never feel like I am a winner?

2 MUCH 2 YOUNG

CHAPTER 4
REFLECTING

I was born in the front room of our council house in Oldbury, near Birmingham, on 5 January 1965, a birthday I share with Vinnie Jones, the ex-footballer and now film actor (not a very useful fact..lol). I am the youngest of five children – three sisters and one brother.

I know that many people have the same story as mine, that is, rags to riches, blah, blah, blah (there are various forms of riches, not only financial ones, I should add). But to understand what has motivated me throughout the years you do need to under-stand my background and the impact it has had on me.

We were poor; we were so poor that we lived in a cupboard in the home of another poor family who were better off than us … lol.

Sorry … I felt an old Monty Python sketch moment coming on … but we did have a dead parrot once … well, more a love bird really that our cat decided to eat. Anyway, we were poor by today's standards, although not the poorest family in our street.

This was the swinging sixties and Britain was just starting to really prosper again after the effects of the Second World War. The war had depleted the resources of the country and the 1960s was the decade when people really felt that things were on the up. At this time, though, only a few people had very much in the way of true monetary wealth.

My parents both worked, my mum part-time at my Uncle Phil and Aunty Vi's grocery shop about a mile from our house and my dad at a steel foundry a couple of miles away in Smethwick.

We did not have much, but we always had food on the table and clean clothes on our backs. Some of my earliest memories are of being very happy, although as a young child I may not have seen the hardships for what they actually were. We did not have a car, no family 'up our street' (my dialect comes through sometimes) did. In fact, I can't remember actually travelling in a car until I was about four or five years of age.

One of my earliest and most vivid memories is of me sitting in the gutter on the pavement outside our house and watching the rag and bone man coming down the street. For those of you who may not know who or what this is, it was a person who used to collect old rags, metal items, and so on from houses and then take them to a merchant and sell them on. He would come down the street and shout out 'rag and bone' over and over to attract the attention of people in the houses, who would then bring out any old items to him. If you were lucky and had enough items they might even give you a live goldfish in a plastic bag for your trouble. However, the goldfish never lasted that long as people could not afford a fish tank to keep them in and they would run out of oxygen in the plastic bag and die.

I never remember having a goldfish, most of our clothes were utilised as 'hand me downs', I think. This is what happened when you had older brothers and sisters, clothes would be worn until you grew out of them and then they would be stored until someone else grew into them. By the way, *no* I did not have to wear my older sisters' clothes.

The rag and bone man had a horse that pulled his cart that would be stacked very high with heavy items. I used to be mesmerised by the height of the items stacked and wonder how the poor horse could actually pull the cart. I still think that this was cruel, but obviously the ragman needed to get as much onto his cart to ensure his day was worthwhile, a sort of 'economies of scale' you could say. I realise now that even as a child I used to think a little too deeply about things, something that has remained with me throughout life and sometimes stops me from being more spontaneous, I can be a little boring and predictable.

I just want to take this opportunity to stress what a struggle it must have been for our family and other families in those days.

Occasionally we would have an ice-cream man come down the street. Playing a really annoying and very loud recorded chiming tune, such as the 'bells of saint Clements', to attract children's attention. Children would then pester their parents for money to buy an ice-cream cone or iced lolly, me included.

When I used to watch the film *Chitty Chitty Bang Bang* with my daughter I always used to wonder if the inspiration for the ice-cream/sweet salesman scene, where the child-catcher entices the children, came from *Ian Flemings* own memories of an ice-cream man down his street. I doubt it very much, though.

So, another of my memories is looking up at the ice-cream man in the window of the van and asking him if he had any broken bits. Broken bits were pieces of ice cream cone that had been damaged and were not sellable. Occasionally, if I was lucky, he might actually give me some and, if even luckier, break a few centimetres from the bottom of a cone and put a dash of vanilla ice-cream into it.

You see, we had no money for such luxuries and therefore had to be creative and a little bit manipulative. I stood there, about three years old, with my then blonde hair and my blue eyes flashing, longing expression on my face and trying to tug at his heartstrings. Imagine if you would, the Puss-in-Boots character from the film *Shrek*, when he removes his hat and looks up with his big sad eyes ... they modelled that character on me...lol! I wonder if I should implement the same strategy as this when asking for funding for a new project....hmm.

That ice-cream tasted so very good; no ice-cream has tasted that good since. In those days you had to appreciate and savour every moment of a luxury item. I am sure the ice-cream man did not retire a rich man from the amount of money he made (or did not make) from our poor street. Life was bloody hard back then, has it changed so much or is it just that I don't see it?

Summers seemed to go on forever in those days and my sisters, brother and I used to spend our entire time outdoors in the street or in our simple garden. Even at a young age it was okay to play in the street alone. We did not feel at risk, as the whole community knew each other and they made it their business to know each other's business. They looked out for one another then; I think you would say that it was 'camaraderie caused by circumstance'. But hey, I am not a shrink, although I have had sessions with one, another story further on in the book.

Winters also seemed a lot harsher than they are now, I am not sure why. Maybe it is global warming or maybe it's because the houses were so bloody cold then, without such things as double-glazing and central-heating. Waking up in the morning and scraping your finger down the inside of the window to find you were touching ice was a common occurrence. We also used to have overcoats thrown over our bed covers to provide added warmth; the days of the duvet with its tog numbers were not yet upon us.

I spent five years at 161 Beeches Road, Oldbury, Warley, West Midlands. Yes, I can still remember the address. To digress slightly, the one thing I have always had going for me is a great memory. I tend to remember things by doing or experiencing them rather than reading and can vividly recollect things from a very early age, as far back as around two years of age.

I had all the usual childhood illnesses, such as chickenpox, but I also remember having pneumonia when I was about three years old and I am sure I was gravely ill with it.

The house was owned by the council, as were all the houses in our particular area of Birmingham. This meant that rent had to be paid each week to a man who would come round door-to-door, collect the money and sign the rent book to say it had been paid. I think my mother was very good at juggling her house-keeping money and always made sure this was paid on time. Having funds to pay meant we did forego the tradition that other families had of hiding behind the sofa when then door was knocked to avoid the rent man; we only hid behind the sofa when watching *Doctor Who* instead.

I sometimes drive my car past the house I was born in if near to the area. I do this just to remind myself where I have come from and to 'ground' myself again. I recently took my stepchildren, Rose and George, past the house to show them where I was born. They were amazed that I was actually born in the front room (George calls it the front window ... always the joker) of a house as most people are born in hospital in this day and age. Also, I think it hit home a little how privileged they are to live where they do and in the environment we provide for them, although as children I am sure any such feelings will be short-lived. I do not think this was a bad thing to do, just to try and remind them sometimes that we are privileged and lucky.

Memories are strange things you know, the things you do and do not remember. I do, however, distinctly remember having my bed in the downstairs front room of the house while I was very ill with the aforementioned pneumonia.

Basically the downstairs of our house had two rooms, the kitchen (come-dining-come-sitting-room) and the front room, or the 'best room' as it was always known. This room was hardly ever used, except at Christmas time or other special occasions. We used to have a six-foot long, floor-standing cabinet unit made of wood. It had an integral 45' and 78' record player and radio, collector's item now I would imagine. At Christmas time I can distinctly remember my dad playing his records while we were sitting reading Christmas annuals (children's comics like the *Beano* and *Dandy* that had been put into a bumper edition), and playing with the few gifts that mum and dad could afford to give us.

On birthdays he would put on an old 45' record by Lonny Donnigan; side B of the record was 'Happy Birthday to You', which we sang with much vigour to the person whose birth-day it was, and then followed this with side A, 'My Old Man's a Dustman', also sang with vigour. It became a sort of family tradition.

In my early pre-school years my Nan used to come round to our house and look after me while my mother went out to work. All families lived near to their relatives in those days and the saying was that they lived 'around the corner'; in our case, they actually did.

My Nan was a wonderful lady; she was about 5ft tall and quite plump with dark hair which went grey later in life. She had a very hard life before and during the Second World War, with a father who beat her hard on several occasions, once breaking her nose. I later found out that he was the undefeated boxing champion of India for the army. He later had something to do with the training of a British boxer named Randolph Turpin. Randolph made it into the history books by beating Sugar Ray Robinson to become the middleweight champion of the world in 1951, a title he held for sixty-four days before Robinson won it back. Randolph later committed suicide at the age of thirty -seven in 1966, but has since been inducted into the American International Hall of Fame. The internet is such a wonderful fact finding tool don't you think?

This does not detract from the fact that my great grandfather was a bruiser of a man, of Romany gypsy origin, who later in life lost a leg when running for a bus. Buses in those days had a footplate; this was open, without a door, and you got on and off the bus at the footplate. Apparently he was running for the bus as it was moving and slipped when trying to get on the footplate and fell under its wheels; justice, don't you think?

I do remember him driving a blue, three-wheeled disabled car which he later committed suicide in by driving into the lock of a local canal. Obviously he had some issues throughout his life; maybe he should have written a book to expel his demons? Really I should not gloat, but this really does look like poetic justice for all of the hardship he gave my Nan and great grandma.

I had started school at the local infants' school, Moat Farm, located at the end of the street. I had been there for about six months, when one lunchtime I walked out of the school gate to go home for dinner only to find my mother stood there with Norman.

Norman was our 'bread man', or so I thought. In those days you had nearly everything delivered to your door by salesmen: bread, milk, fizzy drinks, etc. The concept of super/hypermarkets did not exist back then; we had local shops and deliveries instead.

What I understand now is that my mother used to go out dancing some evenings for a break from her mundane life looking after five kids, home and husband (She married very young).

She had met Norman at one such dance evening. They had been seeing each other quite a while before my mum decided to leave my dad in favour of him.

She put me into the car, an old Ford Zephyr (yes, he had a car, possibly the first one I went in) and told one of my friends to tell the teacher I would not be returning to the school today or ever. My youngest sister, Gillian (four years older than me), was already sitting on the backseat of the car when I got in and I remember huddling up to her as we drove away, not understanding what was going on.

I probably asked many questions, but to me everything else on that day is a blank and a blur in my memory, apart from passing tall trees and seeing cows and sheep in farm fields, a very rare sight for me coming from a built-up city area.

Trauma does that sort of thing; it makes your body produce chemicals that protect you from harm. In my case this is my 'out of body' thing I regularly get in times of stress. But as a child you do not understand this and what you feel is numbness or real fear.

I now realise that events like this stay with you all your life and either make you stronger as a person or weaken you. In my case I think it resulted in a mixture of both: I am stronger because of it, but it also made me insecure and shy. These are things that I still suffer from, as you well know by now.

CHAPTER 5
WALKING WITH GIANTS

It has been a while since I sat down and contributed anything to the book. I am realising that the innovation award has slightly altered my working life. Yesterday I attended a panel event where several other invitees and I debated who we felt had been 'Agenda Setters' in the technology business arena during the past year. This is something I would never have been invited to before and to be honest I was quite nervous about attending it.

Many of those around the table were seasoned professionals of some note, and me, well, I just felt like I was walking with giants. I felt I contributed to the debate well, but had no idea who some of the names put forward to be nominated were.

Today I was sent the final list of nominees compiled from yesterday's meeting and I have sat down, researched the names I knew nothing about and some of these have now made my final vote.

My whole perception of the industry I am in is beginning to alter. I find myself looking further afield for something stimulating for me to get my teeth into. The year 2005–2006 in my opinion has not been a good year for technological breakthroughs. I see the big corporations just shoving the same old muck out to the masses, all be it with a different branding. Such companies are stifling the creativity that is out there. Where are all the new faces and ideas that we need to move humanity forward?

Yes, I admit it to myself; my current job has become boring. I have to stimulate my brain cells with other activities, such as writing this book, to keep me from banging my head firmly against the wall for some excitement. I used to love what I did in the early days of my career...............

I left high school without notable qualifications. The words 'Young, you will never amount to anything of worth' were still ringing in my ears as my parents decided that I should go to college. Colleges in the UK are not like those in the United States. UK colleges, in my opinion, are for those people who do not attain the exam results needed to get into university, or who cannot afford to attend university. This is possibly even more of an issue now with even the poorest of students having to saddle themselves with debt to get through university with grants not being as prevalent.

In my case, I later found out that if I had not been so bored at school, maybe I would have got to university, but that may be an excuse many of us can use.

I studied for one year at North Worcestershire College in Bromsgrove. The college was good, but I was not that interested in the engineering subject that I found myself doing. You see, at this period in my life I still did not have a clue what I wanted to do. My daughter Charlotte is very much like I was, she has no idea what she wants to do and is just entering her last year of high school, with her final school exams looming.

Charlotte is not academic; I have never considered myself to be academic either. Rose, my stepdaughter, is academic and I am sure she will be entering university in a few years' time, but I am also sure even she will not have a clue what she wants to do as a career.

In my opinion, when we are young the world is a big place, but we are totally focused on what is happening in our 'personal space' at that given moment in time, rather than the fact that things move on and we have to move on with them. That is all fine and well and is part of the development towards adulthood that we all have to experience.

My engineering course was scheduled to run for one year and was a requirement for moving onto a further year's study for the HNC (Higher National Certificate), a bit like an 'A' level. The course was the only one available to me due to my exam results being so poor.

I have to digress for a moment again as I have just thought of something; if engineering was the only course available to me with my terrible exam results, did this mean that engineering at that time was considered to be inferior as a career? Bloody hell! Brunel and the other great Victorian engineers would turn in their graves if they knew engineering was being perceived like this!

Okay, back to what I was saying. As part of the course we would occasionally be taken to various small laboratories and workshops around the college campus to learn things about combustion engines, and so on. One day we were taken to the computer laboratory. This comprised of a number of 'green screen' Apple personal computers; state of the art for that day. A young chap was sitting writing something on the green screen using a keyboard; he informed us that he was writing a computer program to work out the probability of numbers. I looked at the letters and numbers on the screen and they meant nothing to me, but I was intrigued to understand more about this strange machine and the language used. I later realised the language being used was Beginners All-purpose Symbolic Instruction Code (BASIC).

My college year ended and I achieved the required pass in the subject, or at least I assume I did; it was a long time ago.

The early 1980s was a time of high unemployment in the UK. This time spawned many things, including such bands as The

Specials and UB40 (taken from the name of the slip you were given at the unemployment office to claim money), something I knew all about as I had to do this for a short time myself.

I needed sponsorship from a company to allow me to move to the next part of my HNC, but with companies laying people off due to the recession, there was no way I was going to get this. Things looked bleak for me; I had no prospect of getting a job and no qualification to talk about.

At the time, the government were running a project called the Youth Opportunities Programme (YOP). Basically, if you were below the age of eighteen, prospective employers could take you onto their books at the rate of twenty-five pounds per week for a period of one year. Many of the people of my age thought that this was really a way of companies getting 'slave labour', that is, giving menial tasks to the YOP employees, and therefore they would not take the places.

As I was approaching the age of eighteen, with no prospects, I visited the Job Centre, who suggested that I took part in a YOP. They told me about a company called ACT Maintenance Limited that was looking for a booking-in clerk. ACT stood for Applied Computer Techniques. The word 'computer' grabbed my attention, although I had no idea what a booking-in clerk did. An interview was arranged for me.

On the day of the interview my parents insisted that I wore a suit. I was a little reluctant about the suit, but they pushed the point that if I looked respectable then I stood a chance in the interview. I attended the interview with Doug Ross, a pleasant chap, who later had a nervous breakdown at his desk and had to finish work, I seem to remember.

I look back now and know that my parents were right about presentation, something I am still very aware of today. My interview did go well and I was given the YOP position and duly started the following Monday as a booking-in clerk

ACT maintenance was a division of an up and coming company in the world of personal computers, primarily selling a PC called the Sirius 1 (Victor 9000 in the US). My job was to take the details of machines being brought in for repair, unpack the items and place them in a queue for the technicians to take into the workshops. Cleaning the floor was also part of my duties. Earth shattering work, don't you think?

Over a period of weeks I got to know people and watched what they did and learnt from them. At the time the Sirius 1 had a power supply problem with a resistor failing in the power supply unit (resistor in position R12, as I seem to recall; I found out at this time that I had a good memory as well). I noted the fault and what the technicians were doing to rectify this from what they had written on the job sheets. I kept hounding them, telling them that I could fix these. One lunchtime they conceded and let me have a go. To their surprise, I did fix one and they carried on showing me other things during other lunchtimes, such as diagnostic tools and how to solder circuit boards, and so on.

Within six months I was offered a full-time position as a technician on a higher salary. It's worth pointing out that ACT later became Apricot Computers Limited, who at the time were the second biggest PC manufacturer in the UK, behind IBM and ahead of Compaq, and who also introduced the first sixteen-bit personal computer in the UK.

During my time at Apricot I learnt how to repair PCs, printers, photocopiers and hard disk units. I distinctly remember not having many manuals to learn from, everything was ground breaking then. Fore example one day I had a pile of broken small photocopiers dropped on my work bench and was duly told to fix them, interesting problem considering I did not have a clue, but I had fun learning.

My claim to fame whilst there was that I held the record for repairing the most PCs in one day without any of them being returned for the same fault. I cannot remember the exact number but it was in the region of thirty. As always, if I am given a challenge, I like to do my best.

I finished my term with Apricot after only two and a half years and ended up in a technical support position with the company.

These were good days; PC technology was a new thing and every day we were seeing new innovations and many of the big companies we now know were just setting out. I saw new items at the research and development stage, went to product launches at the Royal Albert Hall and took part in computing events that were held every January at the National Exhibition Centre in Birmingham, mixing with people such as Bill Gates and Peter Norton who were all vying to promote their own companies and products. I can honestly say that I loved my time at Apricot and the family feeling it had as a growing innovative company.

CHAPTER 6
KIDDERMINSTER HERE I COME

When my parents split up, it also spilt up my family and therefore my world as I knew it. Only my sister Gillian and I went with my mum and her new partner to live in a newly built house located in a town called Kidderminster. My brother David and other sisters Pamela and Julie stayed in Oldbury.

Kidderminster, for those who are not aware, used to be the key area in the UK for carpet manufacturing and produced carpet brands such as Axminster and Wilton. However, the industry is now nearly closed down, mainly due to the popularity of wooden flooring and carpets that are manufactured and imported cheaply from other countries, leaving quite a lot of unemployment in the town.

It's a shame to see a town's bustling economy go downhill in such a way. But if one thing is inevitable in life, then it is change. I am going to get a little bit business-like now:

In my opinion the art of change is being able to predict when it might happen, what the cause and effect will be and a way to mitigate the risk to you or a business. This is a bit of a black art and I think that people either have the 'gut instinct' needed to tackle a changing environment or they do not.

I talk about change in this way because it is something I have experienced all my personal and working life. I once read a great book called *Who Moved My Cheese*, by Spencer Johnson, MD. I would advise anyone who is involved in change to read this short book as it really does tell you what sort of character you are when it comes to change, for example do you panic and refuse change or do you embrace it? I think that my personal trait is to neither refuse nor embrace change. I accept that change is inevitable and just get on with it, hitting the problem head on, as it were. I have effectively been made redundant on two occasions during my working life and this is the way I tackled it at the time.

Being a business leader is about change and what I have explained might be one of the reasons I am successful, or I hope I am successful; who am I to judge?

Number Twenty Silverstone Avenue, Kidderminster, Worcestershire, a newly built house, was our new home. My mum and her new partner must have had this planned for a while; they would have needed time to find the house and place a deposit on it. The only trouble was that it had hardly any furniture, as money was still so tight for them.

It was pointed out to me recently that with the advent of colour television many ladies in the family started seeing the colours and aesthetics used inside the homes of such sitcoms as *Peyton Place*, a US daytime soap opera programme. This caused a flood of orders for furniture, wall coverings and carpets that meant that waiting lists could be anything up to three years for some items! So, do we have to blame the invention of the colour television for the garish designs that we had in homes in the UK during the 1970s? Sorry, but I just love useless bits of information.

On reflection it must have been hard for them, starting a new home, my step-dad taking on two children (he had none prior to this), a new town, and so on.

The house itself was a three-bedroom semi-detached and was in the middle of a building site as this part of Kidderminster was just being developed as a housing estate. This was the 1970s and the time of strikes, the three-day working week and inflation gone mad. I am not that interested in politics, but what I can say is that in business and general life you have good and poor leaders. However, poor politicians can do a lot more damage on a much wider scale and this era became a prime example of it.

I can distinctly remember spending nights in the lounge with only candlelight because the power supply workers were on strike for higher wages or such like. This was also a problem for warmth as we had an electric fire that was also cut off. I hated that bloody fire and had reason to as it burnt my bum on two separate occasions. You might well ask how this happened; well, we did not have central- heating so I often got changed into my pyjamas in front of the fire on cold winter evenings. When you are small and facing away from the fire and bending down to pull up your pyjama trousers, well you can guess the rest. Suffice to say, having grid patterns from the fire guard burnt into your bottom isn't much fun.

As my local area was a literally a building site, I spent many an hour playing army games in the trenches that were dug out for foundations of new houses. These games were played with my then friend Phill, yes another Phil but with a double l. Phill moved into our street a few weeks after me, with his parents and a slightly older brother. They also came from an area near to where I used to live in Oldbury – Warley. Obviously the family were looking to build a better life for themselves in a more rural location. Phill and I are still friends to this day. I do not see him much, but we both know that if the chips were down we would come rallying to each other's aid.

My first and consecutive days at my new school were a bit traumatic for everyone concerned. Franche infant school was about three miles from where I lived and I had to be taken to school by my step-dad in his delivery van on route to work. I think he was still working as a bread man at the time but he did have a few varied jobs in the 70s including; working for a consumer meat products company, a milkman, a welder and he also did a spell at Longbridge (unfortunately now shut down) making cars.

The school had a white farm type gate at its entrance and as I was ushered through the gate I would start to panic, cry and scream quite badly, freaking out really. I would climb the gate trying to escape, usually with a teacher tugging me down, reassuring me and dragging me into a classroom. I remember my mum crying too on the occasions she had to drop me off.

To this day I still cannot understand that people didn't appreciate what I must have been going through. Looking back, the school represented my first school, Moat Farm, the one I was taken from and I obviously associated this with the threat of being left behind like my other sisters and brother were.

Children become mentally scarred from trauma in their lives and I am no exception. These memories are what later drove me to behave in the way I did with my own daughter during my own divorce. More of that later.... Yes I know there are a lot of later ons in the book; we will get there eventually, I promise.

By the way, after going through various things in my more recent life, I do not blame my mum, dad or step-dad for anything that happened in my early or later life. I understand that things get complicated; people change over time and with these complications might come the unexpected and the traumatic. However, it did take me a long time to realise this and also a little bit of professional counselling. I also now think that writing this book is becoming part of 'closing' these matters off in my mind.

I did settle down at school eventually and when a new infant school was completed nearer to my home I relocated to it, Marlpool first school. I even captained the football team for a match, and even though they placed me in defence and I did not kick a ball all game, the team won a trophy. I think this was a token gesture from my teacher, I was the oldest boy in the school at the time, and had nothing to do with my prowess as an athlete ... lol I was always terrible at football. As my parents both had to work, they could not attend to see this achievement. As a child you never understand why parents cannot come to every school event, do you.

It's amazing now to think that I used to walk home from school, two miles or so by myself or with friends, at the age of seven. Would you allow your children to do that now? Is it a sign of the times, have things really got less safe or are we just more paranoid than our parents were?

An old cliché I know, but the summers were warm and seemed to last forever in those days. We always had plenty to do as children; the housing estate was located very near to farm and marsh land and we used to spend our hours looking for newts in ponds, bird's nests in trees and rolling in freshly cut hay.

One of our favourite summer games was taking large cardboard boxes that we had salvaged from the local shops to a large grassy bank, spreading them out flat, then sitting on them and sliding down the bank. I could not imagine my children doing this now. I am sure they would love it but they are more into MSN and play stations. Something is definitely missing from their lives, don't you think? I wonder what the future holds for their generation; they are very technologically aware and take such technology for granted. I know that many children have hundreds of acquaintances in virtual spaces such as MSN, myspace, bebo and the second life virtual worlds. This also makes me wonder how this might change the future of business.

Are our current business structures stifling creative people? We expect our employees to respond in certain ways and abide by the rules we build around them with the security measures we put in place via policies & procedures. However, our children do not have such boundaries and this could be a real problem for them and us if we do not embrace a new way of working. I am seeing more and more examples of younger people not taking positions within organisations because they are not offering flexibility in the working environment. Although people will always consider the overall package on offer when taking on a position, this flexibility factor is now starting to count toward the 'wooing and retention' of these people.

They use different devices for various things; we use mobile phones to talk on, whereas they see mobile phones as a text device. They make virtual transactions in virtual space; this is making such places as 'second life' a very lucrative business environment.

This leads me to wonder if in the future our children might make business deals within such spaces, that is, meeting with someone 'in the space' and this then resulting in a real world business transaction. Wow, this is getting a bit deep.

Because children do not interact vocally so much I also wonder if nature will make changes. Just think we could have children being born without tongues, with their thumbs repositioned to allow them to text faster…lol.

CHAPTER 7
CIO

So I AM considered to be a CIO. To be quite honest, I dislike this term and am planning to say so at a convention I am speaking at in a few weeks' time. The term implies that I am a manager of information, and this is only one aspect of what IT directors/heads of IT/CIOs do.

I think me saying I dislike the term may be a little bit controversial as the audience will comprise of my peers and many of them have the CIO title, but what the hell! You might as well say what you feel because being 'establishment' can be so boring at times.

As I write these paragraphs I am in the current position as head of IT operations for Amtrak Express Parcels Limited. I have been in this position for nearly four years and I think I have been quite successful. Amtrak is a good company with good people, but has limited scope for my own growth within the business. The parcel delivery sector in the UK is very competitive and margins are tight; this means that every piece of work I undertake has to either reduce cost or improve revenue within a very short timeframe. I am okay with this requirement and it has made me be very creative in some of the things I have done, but it would be so nice to have a little cash to do other things with. I know I could make so much more of a difference.

I have a team of about twenty-five people working with me. The original team was larger, but having to make cost savings has reduced the head count.

The one big lesson I have learnt at Amtrak is that people and the management of them can be a real nightmare at times. I have had to make redundancies and pressure people into accepting compromise agreements. To me this is just business and I am sure many of you are aware that in this day and age the probability of you being made redundant in your working life is very high. However, for some reason people working for you do not understand this and take it very personally, even though you explain it to them.

To date I have had one ex-employee try to take the company to tribunal, but worse than this they tried to seek damages from me personally for various things they said I discriminated against them for. *Moi?* Discriminate? I am probably one of the last people who give a damn about age, race and gender. As long as you can do a job well and deliver what I ask, that is all that matters.

I have also had another employee get very vindictive and try to tarnish my reputation by sending emails to the managing director and posting remarks about me in the on-line press. I have had abusive phone calls at all times of the day and night, and so on. They really should get on with their lives; dwelling on the past must be emotionally frustrating and I do feel sorry for them.

I commenced my employment with Amtrak at the same time as I commenced my split from my ex-wife. This might sound like a mad thing to do, but for me it made perfect sense.

You see, I am a little bit of a planner and when you are a planner you also tend to extract yourself from a situation and become very rational about things; back to the protection mechanism thing I had in my early days when my parents split. This protection mechanism is a strange thing; I am like Dr Jekyll and Mr Hyde, although I do not think I have a bad alter ego. Whenever I am under immense emotional pressure something clicks and I will go 'out of body', leaving the gibbering idiot behind, and become a planner, a rational thinker.

My rationale at this time was to keep myself as near to Charlotte as I could. Therefore, I decided to give up my own consulting business that I had done for 7 years, as this was keeping me away from home. So Amtrak was a means to an end in my personal life. I will always thank my superior for sticking by me at a very difficult time in my life, and I think that the loyalty I feel towards this person is the only thing still holding me at Amtrak.

My life as a CIO can vary; one day I can be sitting signing off boring invoices and the next day I can be attending events such as the 'Agenda Setters Panel', previously mentioned. I have managed to build a good team around me and this now means that I have very little to do except offer guidance to them. I find myself spending more and more time looking for ways to amuse myself, the book being one of them.

Although I hope this book is a good read, I do feel that I am becoming stale and very soon will need to move forward in my working life. I need change in my working day, becoming bored starts to depress me and this is not a good thing for my family who always tend to get the brunt of my frustrations and anxieties.

I have worked in some aspect of computing for over twenty-five years and have seen many changes, some good, and some bad. One thing that still manages to amaze me though is how the strategic consulting community can still manage to re-badge something as 'the next best thing' when the longer in the tooth of us in the industry know it's usually just some older idea/concept that they have suddenly hit on again and which has become flavour of the month; a cash generator.

I have seen personal computers develop, digital watches become more function rich, pocket calculators actually get small enough to get in your pocket, technology getting smaller &

smarter, the advent of mobile phones and the World Wide Web. All these things are considered to be everyday items and must haves by Generation X-Box, as children might become known.

My first experience with a computer game was 'ping'. This was a table-tennis game, comprising of two paddles, a net and a ball on the television screen in black and white. It was my Christmas present when I was about ten years old. It was in a black box called 'Grandstand' that plugged into the television aerial socket. How things have moved on ... well the graphics have got better anyway.lol.

I now consider myself to be at the top of my career ladder. Yes, I could go to a larger, more successful company and probably earn more money, but I would still have the CIO tag and do similar things. Thus, in the IT world, I already have the top title.

To this point I have given you an insight into my early years and my early working life. I plan to take you further into my teenager years and more about my working life, but I want to point out that I never actively planned to be at the top in IT. It may look like it when you continue reading, but I think like many things in life it is seventy per cent down to luck. Don't tell that to any prospective employers though, just tell them Phil is exceptional – read his book! ... ☺

You can be good at what you do, but you also need the breaks.

I was lucky and had them and I am very grateful to whoever is watching over me. I would like to think that this might be my Nan or granddad. My granddad was a real gentleman and he always seemed to have time for his grandchildren, but we sadly lost him to the big C (cancer) when I was about nineteen years old. He had been suffering for a long time with the illness, never complaining, but he just wasted away. He was six foot tall and in good shape, but he ended up looking gaunt and wasted. This can be a vicious disease and I really hope they find a cure for it one day.

On the evening of his death I had the strangest experience. I was driving past my grandparents' home and I do not remember making a conscious decision to stop and visit them, but I found myself knocking on their door and one of my sisters answered it. She informed me that granddad had just died in his bed and for some reason I was not surprised. The odd thing about this is that I had not planned to stop and I just felt myself being guided to them.

As I think back now I do feel that there are powers in this world that we know nothing about, things which link us together and a road that is possibly mapped out for us. I am not saying that I believe in an ultimate God-like presence, but I personally think that there is definitely something going on.

I am finishing writing this chapter after a few days break from the book. A few things have happened since I last wrote anything. Firstly, the main shareholding venture capital company within Amtrak has just sold up and we now have a US private equity company involved as a major shareholder.

I knew this was on the cards, but what has surprised and annoyed me is that even though I am classed as being a senior member of the Amtrak team I did not know the details until an email went out to all the employees of the company, including me. So I now know where I stand in the pecking order of the company, not at the top anyway.

Secondly, I have attended an interview; the position was IT director for Europe for a large logistics company, no names please. I took the day off work as holiday yesterday and attended the interview, about an hour and a half journey from my home. What became apparent very quickly during the interview was that the company were a little inflexible, for example they expected me to work in Europe for most of the week and then in the office (one and a half hours away) for the remaining day to write reports (obviously these could be written anywhere). I informed them that this did not suit my work/life balance and therefore we agreed that we would not take things further. What a waste of time.

I now firmly try to put my family before work and this position would have totally compromised this. I should count myself as being lucky that I can, to a certain extent, pick and choose positions, a lot of people don't have this luxury.

Well, I have decided I have had enough of being where I am. As mentioned this feeling is mainly due to the cash constraints the company has and therefore I am just baby-sitting the existing operation with a few minor tweaks here and there. Although, it has not helped how I have been treated recently.

Also I have worked out that financially I am worse off this year than I was in year one of my employment with the company. This has been due to the bonuses being awarded to me each year becoming less and less, even though I have achieved all my personal targets and objectives. This is blatantly unfair and with everything combined I have lost the commitment I had to the company.

Enjoyment and reward are two of my core values, and these values motivate me. I also need challenges in my working life, challenges that stretch and push my boundaries otherwise I start to stagnate. I am not the type of person who can remain with a company for ten years or more and sit and take the pay cheque waiting for retirement.

In my opinion a CIO, or whatever we want to call them, has to be a leader and not just someone going through the motions. My IT managers can easily do my current baby-sitting job and therefore I consider myself to be redundant and I am therefore looking to move on. I have always pointed out to my employers that the whole aim of my job is to eventually make myself redundant by putting in the people and processes that allow this to happen. I feel this time has now come.

Something else that has happened is that the presentation that I am due to give (mentioned earlier), has had a lot of interest and therefore the organisers have called me and asked me to give the 'keynote' speech on the subject of 'Innovation'. This made me wobble a bit; I have never given a keynote before and am more than a little bit nervous about it. But I need to push myself forward again and put on a show as I feel it is important to get my name out to a wider audience to potentially assist me to secure a new position.

Fear stops us moving forward. I intend to spend my later life hitting my fears head-on, tackling them and winning. Speaking in public is one such fear that has to be tackled and hopefully conquered.

So anyway, I want to continue to take you through my life. Starting with the teenage years and then through my later personal and working life. So if you have lost interest by this stage, please skip a few chapters or put the book down at this point and go to sleep if you happen to be reading this in bed.

2 MUCH 2 YOUNG

CHAPTER 8
REBEL, REBEL

WE MOVED AWAY from Silverstone Avenue when I was about twelve years old. We only moved around the corner on the housing estate we lived to a pub called the 'Roundhead'. My parents, who were now married, had decided to enter the licensing trade, working for a company called 'Mitchell's and Butlers'. I had moved from infant to middle school by this time and things were okay with me.

By the way, I call my step-dad 'dad'. I started doing this when I was about seven years of age, not sure why, but I think a lot had to do with the fact that I no longer visited my biological father. This was through no fault of my biological father's, it was just circumstance. Therefore, Norman became my full-on father figure.

My mum and dad (step-dad) have always been very hard working and this has been instilled in me. They managed to build the business up in the pub and life was getting better for them, financially that is. However, they never had a lot of time to spend with my sister and me because they were always working; two shifts a day, one at lunchtime and one in the evening.

This meant that we both became quite self-sufficient and I spent an awful lot of time watching television and playing with my friends.

Lots of jobs need doing when you are in a pub and my job was to clean the car park once a week and bottle-up each day. I never did manage to clean the car park each week but I did bottle-up each day and got paid for doing it. The payment was not a lot but it was more than my friends were getting in pocket money and having to work for it each day made me realise its value. Bottling-up was the cleaning down of the shelving and bottles behind the bar, the re stocking of them and then the removal of the empty bottles from bottle bins and sorting them into crates. I hated emptying the bottle bins; they were always gooey and smelly. To this day I do not like having anything dirty on my hands..lol

I have never really been an outgoing sociable person and therefore I have always had very close and tight-knit groups of friends who I trust and can be myself with. My friends at this time were people I had been growing up with on the housing estate and I still see them around even now, maybe not socially as things have moved on and they have their own lives to live.

I did the usual school lessons at this time, that is, Maths, English, and so on, moaning and groaning about everything. I was never great at sports or a great academic, but I got by. I was in the school table-tennis team and was okay at sprinting, that is, one hundred-metre runs, but not longer distances; too lazy maybe.

For some reason I was considered to be 'one of the hardest kids' in the school, an accolade I am not proud of now and wasn't then. Being the 'hardest' meant that people thought you were tough and not to be messed with. I think this came from me being a little estranged when I was at infant school due to my tantrums at the gate and it followed on with me throughout school. This did have its advantages though as I never got any hassle from the other boys in my school year at middle school.

I should point out that I very rarely got into any trouble in school or out. My mother was very strict with me and I knew that her wrath was far worse than anything the school or the police could summon up. I was just a regular kid, doing regular things and life was good. Well things were good until I moved to my high school :-(

High school was a manic experience for me. The main reason for this was that in my final year of middle school the local education authority decided to move what they call 'catchment areas', that is, the area of homes that feed pupils to a particular school. I was due to go to the high school that my sister attended and where ninety per cent of the children I was with at middle school were going to go, but where I lived was outside of this new catchment area and I had to go to another school. Normally this might not have been a problem, but by this time my friendships had slightly changed and I went around with a gang of friends who all went to my sister's school and gangs from this school and my soon to be new high school were bitter enemies. So, I was on my way to a school that everyone was going to hate me for who I hung around with, how scared would you have been? I was terrified!

My first day at high school did not go well. I really did not want to be there. The first thing we had to do was to sit in the sports hall and wait for our names to be called out to find out what classes we were going to be in. An incident happened between me and another boy, as we sat there, cross-legged, on the floor of the sports hall. This set the course for my high school life: downhill and trying to survive.

I am writing about this on the day that Rose has started her first day at high school. She is really looking forward to it and I am sure it will be a good experience for her, unlike my own experiences. She is very sociable and well liked and I am sure she'll enjoy every moment that school life provides. Unlike me, I spent my days ducking and diving, avoiding trouble with the rival gang to ours and I was very happy each day when I caught the school bus home.

In the late afternoons and evenings I would get together with my own gang of friends. We all used to gather at a local park and play football or just sit, smoke and talk. Yes, I started smoking when I started high school (not very big of me, I know). In fact I still smoke even now, but I really do want to give up and have tried a few times without success.

The 'Franche park gang' as we were known, consisted of mainly boys, with a few token girls who hung around with us. The boys were all one or two years older than me and I always felt that they looked after me a little, a bit like their little brother or something. I can see clearly why teenagers of today get involved with gangs as they do afford a level of peer comfort and protection. Although, in my day, gangs were different in that that we did not really get involved in drugs or weapons of any description, it was more of a social gathering.

My best friend at this time was a lad called David Benton. Dave and I did everything together from the age of about fourteen until a few years after I left Kidderminster. We lost contact when I was eighteen, as I did with a lot of people when my parents moved.

I would have been about thirty-seven years old when I got back in contact with my first friend, Phill. He informed me that Dave had died two years previously in a car crash. This was a real shock for me and I regret not keeping in touch and being able to go to his funeral. We had become young men together and experienced things such as our first venture into discos, drink and girls.

Dave was a very vibrant, colourful person and a sad loss I am sure to his family. I hope he is watching out for me like we did for each other back then. I think about him a lot, especially as I get older and understand more about mortality. How depressing am I today?

In high school, like many boys of that age, girls were always on the agenda. I had a few so-called girlfriends but nothing really serious at that age. Kim was in the same year as me at school and had a long-term boyfriend. She was in a higher stream than me as she was more intelligent and I always felt she was a little out of my league.

We did go out with each other for a few weeks when we were fifteen, but this was short lived as I went on holiday and came back to find that she had decided to go back to her ex-boyfriend, I had been dumped! To be honest, I can remember feeling a little crushed by this; she was extremely pretty and I had fallen for her big time in a boyish sort of way. Also, being dumped tends to dent your ego a little and I did have a big ego at this age.

I was about fifteen when I got kidnapped. Yes, you heard me right, *kidnapped*. A gang of youths decided to drive up to me and bundle me into a car and take me for a ride whilst threatening me with a knife to my throat. They pulled up and called me over to the rear window of the car and as I lent through the open window they grabbed my clothes and pulled me in through it as I struggled, then drove off.

As we drove around the streets of Kidderminster, me sat on the backseat between 2 of the gang, they made me empty my pockets as they looked for money. At the time I had a gold and diamond signet ring that had been on my finger for a long time. They tried to remove it, threatening at times to cut it off with a knife that they held near to my throat, the ring did not budge.

I had seen a few of them around and knew that they were trouble. Based on this information, I would not have said anything about it to any of the authorities and I also knew that the ramifications that surrounded 'telling on them' would be huge in terms of taking beatings every day.

However, I happened to be near home at the time of the incident and my mum saw this from the window of the pub and called the police. I told the police that I did not want to take things further but they insisted as some of the people were very well known to them and they wanted them off the streets.

The main people in question were arrested and sent to juvenile prison for a year for kidnapping, an offence that carried a custodial sentence even though they had not tried to ransom me.

As the time neared for them to be released I got more and more worried about what might happen and spent a lot of time trying to avoid areas I thought they might be. This did cause me one or two problems when they were eventually released as they decided to come looking for me and get their revenge. Suffice to say they never managed to do so as I suddenly found I could run faster than any Olympic gold medallist!

I have since heard that one of the people in question kidnapped someone who owed him *drug money* some years later and had tortured him; he went back to prison and has since died from a drugs overdose himself. What goes around and all that!

This book is sounding more and more like *The Godfather*. I can assure you that these were things I just thought were normal at the time and I dealt with them. I am sure that if you have children growing up in today's world, they are also dealing with things that you may or may not have knowledge of and are just as bad. Not wishing to worry you or anything.

As we grew older, my friends did get into trouble with the police for stealing cars and other things. I never did this with them. Like I said, the wrath of mum was always with me. We did all go on camping holidays though, as a group when I was about fifteen to seventeen and these were great days. They were more like road trips and we had some very good times. I have a lot of memories and it turned out that while the others were more interested in drinking and generally hanging out, Dave and I were more interested in music, fashion and girls; in that order.

I followed fashion and mum always encouraged me to look good. I became a Mod in the revival of the late 1970s and also got into 'New Romantic' music and fashion in the early 1980s, although I never wore any make-up. On one such camping trip to Wales I do remember me and Dave being escorted out of the town of Saunders Foot by the local Police. I can't decide if this was because we were dancing on the pool table of a pub or just because our dancing was so atrocious. On another occasion we also found ourselves being escorted out of Belgium, being taken to the port of Ostend to wait for a ferry to bring us back home in the early hours. But, all of these things happened to us because of boyish pranks and high jinks, never anything serious, I would like to point out.

I was about seventeen when I found myself walking back home one evening across the pub car park where I lived. I caught a glimpse of someone coming out of the door of the pub and the next thing I knew I was waking up on the hard floor of the car park covered in blood, dazed and shocked. The man had hit me hard in the face, causing my nose to badly break and pushing it over to one side of my face. Luckily for me, and unluckily for him, I managed to take note of his footwear. You see, I had been in the town centre earlier that day, hanging out with friends, and had seen the man in question wearing these distinctive shoes and as a follower of fashion I must have made a mental note when someone told me his name.

The police were informed of the assault and I had photographs taken and gave a statement. The man was arrested and charged. The reason I tell you this is two-fold. Firstly, good things can come from bad things. I was given criminal compensation money and with this bought my first car. Well I say first car with some apprehension as it was a white Morris Marina 1300, would you call it a car?

Secondly, it bloody hurt! I have had two operations on my nose to rebuild it internally so that I can breathe and to straighten it externally, not pleasant operations I might add and it is still misshapen. But I just can't pick up the courage to have it changed again now.

Anyway, my schooling ended and I left with very little in the way of exam results. I was extremely happy to leave and can look back and gratefully say that I would not wish to go back to that school even now.

I was not a rebel, but did associate with rebels. I did not realise it at the time but this helped me develop the ability to think on my feet and to be quite cunning when it comes to being in awkward situations. I have never resorted to violence to resolve anything and have always had an ability to use words effectively to disarm situations. I think I developed these skills as a direct response to not liking pain.

CHAPTER 9
MOVING ... MARRIAGE AND BABY

In previous chapters I mentioned that my family moved locations when I left college, we moved to a pub in Quinton, Birmingham. What I omitted to say was that my mum and dad a few years after we had moved from Kidderminster lost their job in the pub trade and had to move for a short while to a house in the same area of Birmingham as the last pub they managed.

The problem was that the house did not have enough rooms for me to stay with them and I ended up living with my Nan for about six months. By this time my granddad had past away, a massive blow to the family. I will have fond memories of him for the rest of my days, not as the wasted shell he became with his illness, but as the happy six-foot, fit character that he was.

My Nan had early signs of Alzheimer's disease when I started living with her and regularly locked the door and went to bed of an evening leaving me unable to get into the house. This meant that I spent many a night sleeping in my car outside. I did so without complaint, as I did not want to worry my mum about her condition.

My stay at my Nan's came to an abrupt end when she mentioned to my mum that some money she had been saving had gone missing from her house and she suspected me. I can genuinely hand on my heart; swear that I never took anything from my Nan, only the love that she gave me. I can only assume that the world of darkness that she was approaching had caused her to think like this. Indeed I think the money was found eventually where she had hidden it and then managed to forget the location.

To this day I try to have high standards in my life, with one being that you should not steal. This is also something I carry through to my working life. It is important to ensure that you do not do anything that can be deemed to be theft, for example playing with your expenses etc. By maintaining standards of this sort it means that you lead by example and in no way feel guilty if you have to reprimand someone for their own errors of judgement.

My parents decided to buy a small coffee house in Falmouth, Cornwall and as I had the Technicians job at Apricot I would not be going with them. My aunt and uncle kindly offered to put me up at their house for a small amount of weekly rent. I was glad of this gesture from them, but I felt very lonely at the time, in a strange house with people I did not really know that well.

Also by this time I had met my soon to be first wife. She

worked as an administrator and receptionist at Apricot and we started dating when we were eighteen years of age. I spent a lot of time at her house with her and her parents and I also stopped over at the weekend so that I did not have to go back to my lonely existence at my aunt and uncle's house.

We got engaged and started saving for a house. We were engaged for four years by the time we bought our first house, a small two-bedroom semi-detached 'dormer' style located on a housing estate near to her parents in Kingswinford, West Midlands.

I remember that the house cost £27,000 and pushed us to our financial limits, something that seemed to remain a common theme throughout our marriage, which is, never having any money to speak of. I moved into the house immediately, but Caroline did not. Her parents were quite old fashioned and insisted that she should not move in until we were married.

I now consider that not living together was a mistake because our first year of marriage was a nightmare of arguments and falling outs due to us not really knowing each other and our habits beforehand.

We married when we were twenty-two years old at the village church. Kingswinford used to be a Staffordshire village named in the *Domesday Book*, and the village church was a remainder from those ancient days, even though the village itself had now

2 MUCH 2 YOUNG

grown into a town.

The lead up to the wedding was very traumatic. I had contacted my biological father a few years previously to this and decided to invite him to the wedding, together with his wife. This did not go down well with my mum and step-dad and they refused to come to the wedding. Obviously they had their own reasons for this refusal.

I learnt a major lesson from this period of time that I carried forward to my own divorce and will also carry it through to any weddings my children might have. The lesson is that no matter how upset you are with your ex-partner you must take a back seat and do what the bride and groom want on their special day and also in their lives.

Eventually they did back down and came to the wedding, but I could sense an atmosphere and I also knew that Caroline was very annoyed with them, something she carried through the rest of our marriage by not wanting to be associated with them. As you can imagine this made life very difficult for me.

The wedding plans got bigger and bigger and I felt that I had no input. I felt stifled by the whole thing and, to be honest, as I look back, I did not enjoy our wedding day.

We did not go on honeymoon like other couples did. Two days after the wedding Caroline's mother had to have a kidney removed, this was planned. This meant that Caroline did not want to be far away from her, something I understood. We spent a week in a family friend's caravan in North Wales near Carnarvon and we made the best of things. Watching the European football cup finals for a week on a portable television in a caravan park might be some people's idea of fun, but it is not really mine.

I have vowed that my up and coming wedding will be nothing like that and both Kim and I agree that we will have a certain level of formality to the wedding but will keep the guest list down and the wedding itself a little quirky. We will be honey-mooning in the Bahamas at Sandals over the New Year period. Just a smidgen different from my first wedding then… lol.

Caroline and I did not plan to have children; this happened by accident and in my opinion was the best accident I ever had. However, we were not ready to lose the extra income from Caroline's wage though and this impacted us badly for many years.

Charlotte was born in January 1991 but this in itself did not go smoothly. Caroline was in labour a long time and lost a lot of blood that should have been replaced while she was in hospital via a transfusion. Also, Charlotte was born with a totally dislo-cated hip that was picked up during a routine inspection of her on the morning after she was born. This was not a major prob-lem in itself, but when you have been through hours and hours of labour and then this news is broken to you, you feel like your world falls in and eats you up. I did my usual 'out of body' thing due to the stress, and in my own little protective world that I create in my head, there was no doubt that she would be anything other than fine.

A few days later we all left hospital and settled back into the house. Unfortunately, due to her lack of blood Caroline went into shock as she began to lose more blood on the first evening back and I had to call an ambulance to rush her back to hospital where they gave her a long-overdue transfusion and sorted out the bleeding. I genuinely thought we were going to lose Caroline at this point and I have never been so scared about anything in all my whole life.

The following day I had to take Charlotte to another hospital appointment to have her hips checked by the paediatrician and I was not happy with the way we were treated at the hospital. With all that had gone on previously I felt like the staff were a little insensitive. Charlottes Nan and I had waited for a while to be seen and I had to pop to my car to get a clean nappy for Charlotte, when I got back the specialist had examined Charlotte and told her Nan everything instead of telling me, her dad. I tackled the specialist about this and his manner but he seemed not to care.

We felt we could not wait for the NHS to get around to tackle Charlottes problem as time was of the essence in getting treatment started, fortunately Caroline's parents felt the same and paid for us to have a private consultation with another specialist a few weeks later. Mr Bradish acted quickly and Charlotte's treatment started sooner rather than later. Don't get me wrong, I think the NHS do a wonderful job under the circumstances, but when it is your own flesh and blood that is being made to sit on a waiting list, it soon makes you think about private medical care. Fortunately for us Mr Bradish recognised that we could not afford to pay for the ongoing treatment of Charlotte privately so he added us to his NHS list at the renowned Birmingham Children's Hospital.

Nearly a week later Caroline came back out of hospital and was told to rest in bed. This was the year of the first Gulf War and I spent about a week of that winter sleeping on the sofa in our lounge with Charlotte in her pram, me feeding and changing her while watching television into the early hours of the morning, seeing how the war was playing out.

I look back and think that these times took a lot out of me, both emotionally and physically. Charlotte had to visit the children's hospital in Birmingham every fortnight for about a year and then a couple of times a year until she was four years old.

Her condition was treated by putting her in a full body harness that pulled and kept her legs up to encourage her hip joint to form. I am grateful to the hospital and Mr Bradish for correcting this defect and Charlotte has had no further problems with her hips. She did, however, get a hernia on her belly button due to pushing against the harness and this needed surgery when she was three years old, once she was released from wearing it.

The worst part of her hernia operation for me was when I had to put her to sleep in the operating theatre. She was crying and the nurse asked me to put her on my lap and hold the gas mask over her face. I can assure you that feeling your daughter go limp in your arms, with me hoping and praying that she will wake up again is something I would not wish on anyone. That devastating feeling you get, the lingering idea in your head that you could have been an integral part in killing your own child if she were not to recover from the anaesthetic. I cried.

I moved jobs a number of times trying to earn more money to keep our heads above water. Caroline did not return to work as she wanted to remain with Charlotte and at the time we thought this to be best due to all the running backwards and forwards to hospitals, and so on.

By this time I was working as a Service Engineer, this was very hard work and involved long hours. It meant I was called out at all times of the day and night, including Christmas Day. I had to look for a more sensible job when Charlotte arrived and got a position as an analyst programmer with a small software company located near to home.

We decided to move house even though we really could not afford it. A friend had a nice house that we admired and this became available. We moved to this larger three-bedroom semi-detached house on another estate in Kingswinford.

Finances were becoming a real problem at the time and we very nearly lost the house. I had to take on extra programming work writing financial management software, and I did this work every day into the small hours of the morning for about nine months. At the time we also sold and fitted house window blinds for a national company. Luckily we were young and had the energy to do this, although I am sure that it did take its toll, working every day, night and weekends. Caroline took the sales calls on the phone and arranged appointments for visits; I did the house visits to sell the blinds and then fitted them on weekends once they had been made and delivered to us. We did not make much money from doing this considering the amount of effort we put in.

What all this did teach me was how to sell to the public and that a good customer service offering is very important in business. People buy into people not just a product.

I eventually was asked to leave the software company after 5 years. I say 'asked to leave' but I was actually fired from the company after all those years of hard work for them. I was told that this action was taken because I had been writing software for other people in competition to the company, that is, the financial software I spoke about. This was such a ridiculous statement for them to make! I purchased software licenses from this company and had told my boss who was the owner of the company everything I was doing! I am now more than positive that the real reason for the company doing this to me was because it was not financially doing that well and needed to downsize. This gave them an excuse to avoid a redundancy payment.

I was effectively fired without pay, but after consulting a solicitor, I met with the company's owner and explained to him that I had rights and he had not followed 'due processes. Eventually he agreed to make me officially redundant, but I never did get any redundancy money from him. The shit!

This hit me very hard and taught me a big lesson at the time, some business people are complete bastards and I really needed to watch out for this in the future and not be so trusting.

This whole episode put me into a complete state of panic and I vowed never to put myself in such a position again. We had no money and I desperately had to sort out a new job otherwise we would definitely go under. I did go to the Unemployment Benefits Office but they did not help, as when you are made redundant they do not pay you benefit straight away because they expect you to have money from the redundancy package you received from your previous employer, something I did not have!

I was caught between a rock and a hard place and feeling very low for a while. I woke up each day with the prime objective of getting a job. My job was now to get a job, and I worked from 8am till 6pm every day doing just that. Within two weeks I had secured a position with a large Taiwanese electronics manufacturer as their senior analyst. This just about managed to save the day for us.

Bored yet? The one thing about writing a book is that it makes you think about things you have forgotten and also it is very therapeutic. I tend to find that I write sections of this book when I am feeling a little low, or feeling on a high, or in need of some inspiration for something else – in other words nearly all the time.

Today I have just finished writing my presentation and speech for the forthcoming Triple i convention – a gathering of IT executives from around the UK who listen to presentations from vendors and peers, which is quite well known in the IT community. It is two weeks away but the organisers needed me to send the presentation in today. I have written it and have been through and timed the speech a few times and think I am happy with it. Unfortunately for Kim, little does she know that for the next two weeks I will be experimenting on her by delivering the speech to her at every available opportunity. Oh well, I know she loves me because she is marrying me and that's what love is all about, sharing and giving or boring her to death, or something like that anyway ... lol.

One other aspect of being a CIO is that I am asked to attend many events like this one. One of the things that I am proud to be associated with is that I have sat on the steering committee of Gartners European Midsize Enterprise Summit for a few years now. Basically this event is for senior people in IT from around Europe and brings them together allowing them to network and also be presented to by some of the more innovative companies in the industry. My position on the committee allows me to help shape the event and I am pleased to say that it is going from strength-to-strength.

CHAPTER 10
DIVORCE

It is quite common in this day and age for people to split up and divorce and as a society we now can tend to trivialise this, with one in three marriages ending in divorce (been listening to Radio 4 again). However, I can assure you that it is not trivial and is still painful for me many years on, although the pain does become less.

I was only with the electronics manufacturer for about a year as there were really no prospects for me with them. I decided, and probably due to the nasty experience I had had at the software company, that I was going to be my own boss and map out my own destiny. This was the late 1990s and I saw contracting as my way out of the company I was with and into a better future for my family.

I sold my car to enable me to create a limited company and to provide a little income until I could get my first contract. As luck would have it I got my first contract within two weeks of leaving. It was a programming contract for a well-known Japanese company, located at their offices in Birmingham. I leased a car and struck out by myself, quite scary really when I think back to how I felt at the time.

I was actually quite successful at what I did, but I made a fatal mistake. Contracting can be very lucrative but the more money I made the more we lived up to and beyond our means. I think this had something to do with not ever having any money from the time we bought our first house and it went to our heads – a lot. This also meant that, instead of taking time off after each contract to spend some quality time with my family, I had to carry on continuously working for six years to pay what we owed in debt.

Many of the contracts I had to take were located away from home so I spent a lot of time living in hotels around the country, returning home only at weekends, which I then spent sorting out the finances of the home and company.

I found that Caroline and I were drifting apart and she was building a life without me as I was never around. It was a very lonely existence for me living in hotels and I felt more and more depressed. I am sure it was also unpleasant for Caroline at times to be without a Husband to share daily activities with. Thinking back, I am sure I was near to and was possibly having a nervous breakdown.

At a very low and weak point I met a woman younger than myself and we had a fling. I say fling because it was not an affair as we only met on a few occasions. Unfortunately for me she had other ideas and must have taken a few hints from the film

Fatal Attraction because she decided to write a letter to Caroline giving graphic and somewhat exaggerated details of our meetings. Why she did this I will never know but she did.

I realise now that Caroline finding out was inevitable because even if the letter had not arrived I would have told her about everything. You see, I find it hard to conceal my feelings, and the guilt I felt inside would have inevitably made me tell her as it would have become all consuming for me.

To be honest I think in some way this whole madness was a relief as we were definitely not happy together at this point and I am sure we both felt that things were going nowhere and we were trapped in the circumstance of it all.

One evening, I sat in a Hilton hotel room in Kensington, London; I say room, but it was a suite as I was such a regular customer that they always upgraded me to one of the best rooms. I sat on the bed in this luxurious room alone and broke down in tears; I felt so alone and sobbed uncontrollably. I felt my life was falling apart and that there was no point to anything. I am sure that for a brief instant suicide crossed my mind but a voice in my head dragged me back from the brink, reminding me of my daughter and how it would make her feel if I were not around.

I decided to visit a councillor each week for a month or so. We discussed my current feelings and my past history. Talking to someone really helped me focus on getting through these tough times.

The one question he asked that always sticks in my mind was, 'What do *you* enjoy doing?' Do you know I could not give him an answer; I had always done things for other people and gone with the flow, been the provider. I had never actually been my own person in my whole adult life and I did not know what I enjoyed doing.

This realisation dramatically changed the way I felt about the situation I was in and me in general. I decided I had to split up with Caroline, even though this was something I had vowed never to do due to my own experiences as a child. I also knew, however, that if I did not leave I would go crazy or worse still.

We had just purchased a 'new build' house and at the exact moment we moved into it we placed it on the market for sale. Also, at the same time I closed down my own business and took the position with Amtrak.

I basically lived in a bedroom of the new house, sleeping on the floor in a sleeping bag for a month or so before I found an apartment to rent close to Charlie. Moving out was harrowing but I knew it was for the best as the atmosphere in the house was awful and Charlie was picking up on it.

You may have noticed that I am calling Charlotte, Charlie.

She is not that keen on this but it is better than me calling her *Charlie Bear* like I did when she was a toddler..lol

Even when you discuss and agree things with your ex-partner concerning aspects of a divorce, the minute the solicitors get involved you can guarantee that things will go pear shaped very quickly and cost a fortune. I am sure Caroline's solicitor thought I was earning a premier league footballer's salary in light of the amount of maintenance they were asking for, not only for Charlie but also for her. I do not begrudge paying to support my child, it is my duty, but the amounts involved were ridiculous considering the position I found myself in.

The divorce took two years to complete and I left the marriage with nothing but a lot of credit card debt that was all in my name. Not much to show for fifteen years of marriage, eh.

Remember that advert on the television a few years ago with the man who walks out onto the steps of a casino with his shirt undone, jacket in hand, bow tie hanging down from around his neck and just playing with his car keys, the man who lost everything, I think it was, but he was happy just to have his car. Well this was me, except I was not happy to have just my car and the cloths on my back… lol.

My prime objective during the divorce was to ensure Charlie was not affected too much by our differences. I think we managed to do this. I backed down on a few things to keep the peace, something Kim still gets annoyed about, but only because she cares about me.

CHAPTER 11

KIM

As I MENTIONED earlier on, Kim is a wonderful, loving, intelligent and beautiful lady. I would say that though wouldn't I.

She has now been running her own successful business for over twenty-three years and makes a sensible living from it. I am very, very proud of her and what she does. She is a designer and manufacturer of tailor made sofas and other furniture and I think that the products she produces are really good quality at a great price, something that people can buy and feel good about and regularly do. Convinced you to purchase something yet?

It was during the early part of my split from Caroline when I decided to go on the 'friends reunited' website just to see if there were any of my old friends still around. One of the things I found out as part of splitting up after a period of fifteen years of marriage is that you lose people who were joint friends, especially in my case, as all our friends were originally Caroline's. So this made me 'Billy no mates'.

On the site I noticed Kim's name and dropped a quick email just asking how she was, what she was up to, and so on. I never had any intention of anything developing between us other than our email conversations. Twenty-five years is a long time not to have known someone and I did not know if she was married and did not want to compromise this if she was.

I was surprised when she wrote back saying that she was married with two children, but her husband and her were also splitting up and she was looking for a house for herself and the children.

We exchanged several emails over a number of weeks and it was mentioned in one of them that a school reunion was planned and that we should meet up at it and have a drink.

Well, as you know, I have been nervous at various times in my life and this was no exception, not only because I was about to meet Kim again, but I was also about to meet a number of other people I had known at school.

I expected all the usual things from the event. You know, 'What are you doing now?' and the one-upmanship that goes with people trying to prove that they have done something worthwhile with their lives – all bullshit really.

I booked myself into a local hotel in Kidderminster and started to prepare myself for the evening ahead. We were all to meet at a wine bar in the town centre prior to moving on to a nightclub. I arrived at the wine bar by myself; as I said before,

I had no friends. I saw a few familiar faces in the crowd and talked to them.

I cannot remember entirely, possibly due to my 'out of body thing' happening again due to the stress, if I was first into the bar or if Kim, her sister and her entourage were, but eventually we met.

She explained that she had just moved into her new home that day and said how exhausted she was. She and her husband had physically split up that day! I think from what I can make out that they mentally split up a long time before this physical split though.

The evening was a bit of a flop really, not a lot of people turned up from school and the wine bar was packed out to such an extent it took forty minutes to get a drink. Also the nightclub was at best described as ... well ... Yuk!

However, we did get a chance to talk, even though this was in-between Kim having to look after her inebriated older sister who had managed to make herself quite ill (found face down in the nightclub toilet, so I seem to remember. Sorry for embarrassing you here, Sara). Sara also went to my school and was in the year above Kim and I, I still remembered her from my past as she dated Dave Benton my friend for a short time.

We caught a taxi from the nightclub after saying our goodbyes to everyone. Kim's sister and entourage had already left; I wonder why? ☺ I dropped Kim off at her new home on my way back to the hotel. We pecked each other on the cheek and I continued on. I remember thinking how nice she was and how this all made me feel like a young schoolboy again.

At about 3am my mobile phone rang and it was Kim, she was obviously finding it hard to sleep in her new home. She asked me if I fancied meeting for breakfast in a local supermarket café later in the morning. I said yes and when the call was over I thought how odd it was. I did not get any indication from our earlier encounter that things would potentially go any further. Also, I did become very aware that Kim is quite a shy person and finds it hard to push herself forward, so calling me in this way must have been quite hard for her to do. Bless her little cotton socks.

We met the following morning, but I think the nerves got the better of both of us as we did not really speak much at all. We met in the cafe of a Tesco superstore and had toast and coffee. It was a rainy morning and to be honest I felt a little hung-over. We made awkward small talk and parted company after about an hour. I said I would text her.

A few days later we managed to arrange to go out for the evening on a weekend. This was a slightly tricky time for me as I was still living at the new house with Caroline and Charlie, but as you know I was not actually together with Caroline. So, as we were all still under the same roof this made me feel quite edgy and guilty at times. I never intended to fall into another relationship quite so quickly, it just happened and I am now very glad that it did. It is funny the way things in life work out, it always manages to surprise me.

After a few months I took the decision to move from a rented apartment in Kingswinford to another rented apartment in Kidderminster. I think it was me who decided this, but as I look back I think a little planning and coercing may have been done in the Kim camp.

Kidderminster has always felt like my natural hometown. At this time I really needed the comfort of being somewhere I understood and was still familiar with and also somewhere that was not that far away from Charlotte. Kidderminster fitted the bill perfectly.

Kim and I were going through the same things and I think this made our bond deeper more quickly; we understood how each other felt and were helping each other through these emotional times. I was spending more and more time at Kim's house to the extent that my new apartment was not being used. We decided that I should not renew the lease and I moved in with Kim and the children. I say we decided, but I cannot remember either of us making a conscious decision about this, it just seemed the right thing to do.

Something I have discovered is that Kim will take quite a lot of time to make her mind up about things, but once it is made up she acts very quickly on her decision. We are very, very different people and this can cause some annoyances on both parts. I am more of a worrier and planner and need a kick up the bottom on occasion to get me into gear when not working, something that Kim is getting very good at (to my annoyance sometimes). I also need a lot of reassurance, but this I think Kim finds harder to give as she is very much a self-starter, one who has bags of energy and keeps on going until she finally collapses from exhaustion each evening.

After about nine months Kim sold her house and we jointly brought the house that we are now living in. Being with Kim has been the fastest four years of my life and together we have done more and achieved more than I did in my previous fifteen years of marriage. This is not a bad reflection on Caroline, but it does show that when two strong-minded individuals have the same goals and ambitions they can achieve quite a lot.

We are not only becoming partners in life, but we are now also partners in business. We have just opened a shop in Kidderminster selling Kim's furniture and other items direct to the public.

I am so proud of her for what she has achieved and is achieving. I love her very deeply, not in a fuzzy or simplistic way, but in a very deep, complicated and meaningful way. I know we will have our hard times and arguments, but I also know that this is nothing to how bad things would be if I ever lost her or my new family. I am not an easy person to live with and I am grateful that she understands me a little. I am so looking forward to all my remaining years being spent with her.

By the way, I have been counting and realised I had effectively moved home five times in a two-year period. They say moving home is one of the top five most stressful things to do. I will tell you something; that is a walk in the park compared to doing it five times while going through a divorce, building a new relationship with a new family and having to perform at director level in a new job. No wonder I have started going grey!

2 MUCH 2 YOUNG

CHAPTER 12
WHO RUNS THE BUSINESS?

Okay, I am bored talking about myself; it's time for a quick business focused rant. If you have read through the book to this point, thanks for sticking with it. You will probably have realised by now that I am not the most politically correct person in the world when it comes to keeping my thoughts and opinions to myself, so I have decided to write a small section that addresses that age-old business question: 'Who runs the business? IT, Sales, Ops, the CEO etc?'

This argument has been going on ever since IT started to materialise and flourish in the business arena back in the early 1980s. I am sick of hearing it and I am sick of people harping on about how IT should basically be 'seen and not heard' and remain subservient to the other business functions as it is a service.

Reality check everyone! IT, ITC, technology, whatever you want to call it, in relationship to a business, is not just about giving tools for people to write documents, calculate pay and produce the accounts, as was the case in the early days of computer technology. No! It is much more than this. Let's get it into perspective, please.

Why do you think that CFOs, finance directors and COOs like the IT function reporting to them? They will say it's about cost control as IT costs a lot of money to run and IT also spends a lot of money ... hmm ... what a load of rubbish! I am more than confident that IT executives at my level are able to manage a budget and control costs in line with what the business needs; if we can't, then why employ us!

No, this is about power. Technology is the most strategic part of any business in the twenty-first century and can easily make or break the fortunes of a business or the careers of its executives. The person who controls IT therefore has a vast amount of power; it's a status symbol, like 'my car is better than yours, so I must be higher up the food chain' or 'my manhood is bigger', that sort of thing ... lol.

If you, dear reader, are an IT person, I know that hidden away inside you, you fully agree with what I am saying but are too scared to say so out loud in case the CFO finds out what you think and banishes you to the IT salt mines, or as it is known 'the accounts department' J. But, if you are not an IT person, you will now be ready to strangle me and banish this book to the deepest part of your department's document repository, to be filed alongside your last audit report no doubt.

However, I speak from experience when I say these things. I have often heard sales functions saying that without them we would not have customers and would not sell anything. I have heard operational functions saying that without them we could not move a product and also finance departments saying that without them we could not get the money called in for the product we sold. All of these are reasonable arguments and true, but without IT you could not do any of those things.

When was the last time you saw a sales person in a computer room moving a data router? But we see IT people out on sales calls supporting sales people to ensure that the company can actually deliver what these people promise to the end customer. When have you seen an operations person cutting some development code for a business system? But I have seen and experienced IT people being called upon to physically sort parcels as operations had a lack of staff or have messed up in some way.

The truth is that IT holistically understands the business far better than other functions. If sales decide to implement a new product or initiative we in IT probably know within half an hour the impact it will have throughout every other function and process of the business. This is what we do, this is what we are good at, this is what other functions fear and therefore need to try and control. The idea of the so-called 'nerds' being in control of the madhouse is too much for them to handle ... lol.

So the answer to 'who runs a business?' is quite clearly 'Technology!' I now rest my case; council for the prosecution can now proceed.

Obviously a lot of this previous chapter was 'tongue in cheek', but I hope it made you think a little.

CHAPTER 13
SO WHAT NEXT?

So DID YOU think you were going to buy a book about how to become successful as a CIO? If you did, maybe you should have read the preface of the book, as no one can teach you this.

People in business are either good or bad at what they do depending on what drives them. Money can be a driver, maybe due to a background of never having any or maybe success has been instilled in someone from an early age. Other things can also drive people such as the need for status, but this is usually more to do with some underlying anxiety created by a need to be wanted.

The common factor in success, in my opinion, is the history and background of the person. If you look back into their past then you may find hardship, general inspirations and something that has triggered the drive that they now have in them. I am no exception to this and have been through a lot leading up to this forty-two year point and I am sure will go through an awful lot more in the years to come. Although I would rather they are nice things ....please.

If you were to ask me to qualify what drives me I would have to say, to be a provider to my family, to be the best I can be as a person, fulfilling my full potential and to be respected by others. Not a tall order then, really..lol, maybe climbing Everest might be an easier task, but I don't like heights.

I have no idea what the future holds for my family or me, but I am sure it will be a continuation of the same roller-coaster ride I have been on all my life. I have learnt a lot about myself over the years and hope to keep learning and becoming a more stable and better person. I can now truthfully say, that on more days than not, I am very happy.

What are my ambitions at the moment? Well, apart from the obvious things like marrying Kim and helping my children grow up to be good people, in the short term I would like to change my job to something more fulfilling. I would also like to help my local community in some way. Finally, I would like to retire to a life of playing golf and holding hands on a park bench with Kim and feeding bread to the ducks with our grandchildren.

I am still continuing my own journey of self-exploration and have just secured the services of a 'personal and career development coach', Robin. I have done this for two reasons. Firstly, I have no idea, not a clue, on how to move my career to the next level or in a direction that I choose; and secondly, I still have issues and baggage from the past that I need to work to free myself from and I need to be taught how to do this.

I met Robin on ecademy.com and have been through a few sessions with him to date. I have learnt that our personal learning should never stop and I would highly recommend any person who has reached 'a fork in the road of life's journey' to seriously consider this form of development – it does help.

Writing this book has been very therapeutic and I have learnt a lot about myself. However, I also recognise that I need expert assistance at times. After all, everyone has something they need help with. Do you?

2 MUCH 2 YOUNG

EPILOGUE

JUST A FEW, brief, hot off the press news items before closing. These are things that have happened since I last wrote in the book months ago now …

Firstly I married Kim at our local registry office on the 23rd December 2006. This was a fantastic day and I will remember it all my life. All the people I wanted to be there were and it made the day very special to me and my wife Kim Johnson-Young.

Remember I told you about my high school, Wolverley High, earlier in the book, the one I did not really make the most of and where I felt terrified most of the time? Anyway, it seems that they want me to be guest speaker at a presentation evening this year for pupils who have achieved 'A' levels and other merits. They want me to give a motivational and uplifting talk about achievement, and going for your goals.

As you can imagine, I smiled to myself when I read the invitation. The boy who heard the words 'Young, you will never amount to anything' and had carried them with him as baggage for years … ha!

Since writing the above paragraph, I have now taken part in the evening at the school and to be honest it was nothing like I expected and my opinions have changed about the 'ha!' thing. Entering the school brought back some good rather than bad, memories and the Governors and Headmaster were very nice to Kim and me. I handed out the envelopes to pupils receiving end of year exam results and achievement awards and shook each of their hands congratulating them. Doing so made me feel very old.

I gave a fifteen-minute motivational talk based on everyone having the 'X-Factor' and going for your dreams. I think it was well received and I felt very humble and privileged to have potentially been able to help shape the future of some young person in the audience. You live and learn, as they say. It was great to have Kim with me, to listen to me perform and to see the other side of who I am and not jus the husband bit.

I have also finally regained control and empowered myself once more by resigning from my position at Amtrak. I have no position to move on to and this is a big risk for me and my family, but if you read the Appendix and see my core values you will find 'enjoyment and reward' being two of them. I am neither enjoying nor feel I am being rewarded correctly for what I do, therefore I have worked over the past four years to make myself redundant and I place myself in the hands of those people watching over me once again.

Officially I had to provide three months' notice, but I provided four as I always feel it is best to be professional about these things. However, after coming back to work since resigning, getting married and my honeymoon, things have changed dramatically at the company.

Amtrak went into administration and was purchased by a consortium of investors within a very short time. I attended a meeting to be told of this by the consortium that intends to run the business 'hands on'. I think it came as a bit of a shock when they were harping on about the importance of technology in the business, as I piped up to inform them I had resigned a few months previously.

The interesting thing here is that, although they realise how important IT is to the business, they did not make any attempt to secure my services. Instead they confirmed to me that I was a 'cost-saving' that they had not predicted – poor them.

So for about four weeks I continued to be the figurehead of IT in the business until one day I sat in a senior management meeting where I was to give my report to the new management team. The managing director let me give my report and then informed everyone that he had asked two IT managers to provide a proposal for how they would run the department when I leave, news to me I thought! Do not get me wrong; this was not sour grapes on my part, I just expected a little decorum and professionalism, and it would have been good to be informed about this as they were still reporting to me.

The following day I called the two managers into my office and asked what was going on, to be informed that they had been working on a lot more things than I knew about and were told not to tell me. Surprisingly they then decided to start implementing *their* plans immediately after leaving my office; this had the net effect of effectively making my position untenable. I felt like that chap in Tiananmen Square in 1989, you know the one trying to hold back the tank. I did look at my calendar to see if it was the first of March 'et tu brute', with me being Caesar on the steps of Rome ... lol.

The point here is that I do not have a problem with people planning my transition, but I do have a problem with not being involved in the planning of it. I have values and try to be professional; I just wish other people would try to be the same. I now call this my 'Mutiny on the Bounty' day and I know who Fletcher and all the main players are. I was set adrift in a boat without a paddle...

During this very surreal time I did manage to formulate my future plans a little. I decided to create my own consulting company and have named it Johnson-Young Associates Limited. I chose the name in celebration of Kim's new posh-sounding surname. We ditched the idea of 'Young' as her surname as it sounded rather like a Chinese takeaway if you said 'Kim Young' quickly when answering the phone…go on try it.

As a further update since the above, I have now been self-employed once more for nine months and have carried out two successful assignments for large companies. I have however taken time off when needed and am living within my means, unlike last time. A lesson learnt, I feel.

My daughter Charlie finished school and is now doing a modern day apprenticeship at a children's nursery school. I am not sure that she will be a nursery nurse forever, or how I feel about it really. However, when I look back at my own career I have to keep in mind where I started (cleaning the floor) and encourage her to progress at whatever she wishes to do in life.

Remember that nightclub that I went to with Kim on the night we met again? Well, Kim has just landed the contract for redesigning the interior. Funny how things turn out, don't you think?

By the way, I have now managed to stop smoking. I have put on a stone in weight but at least I can now breathe, but can't walk due to my weight ☺

Kim's sister Sara is at this moment in time dating my old friend Phill's older brother. If this gets serious I could end up being related by marriage to Phill, what a weird and wonderful world we live in…eh.

2 MUCH 2 YOUNG

I hope you have enjoyed this short book and if you meet me out and about, please feel free to stop me and have a chat. I am a nice chap really, a bit wacky, sad, dull and manic at times, but nice.

Do you cry at chick flick films? Or is it only me? ... lol.

'The future is ours for the taking ... but for the sake of my poor head & heart... please keep it **SIMPLE.**'

APPENDIX A
OBSERVATIONS & VALUES

I HAVE THOUGHT ABOUT this long and hard whilst writing the book and originally decided not to try and provide many tips except as part of the text if applicable. However, I think I have space for a few of my summarised observations on working life and life in general:

Core values: Work out what your own personal core values in life are. Core values are the foundations on which we live our lives and measure ourselves against. Some of my core values are:

+ My family must always come first
+ I must enjoy what I do
+ I must be rewarded appropriately for what I do
+ I must remain professional at all times
+ I must treat people with respect and expect to be treated in the same way.

Once you have mapped out your values, occasionally stop and benchmark yourself against them. If any of your values are being compromised, you should seriously reconsider what you are

2 MUCH 2 YOUNG

doing and take corrective action. If you do not do this you will most certainly be on a downward spiral and will not be enjoying your life as you should. Seriously, we are only on this planet for a relatively short time!

Dreams: Everyone has dreams and ambitions. These can be deep down within us and hard to see at times, but we do have them. You must reach for these dreams and let no one put you off. Remember, 'Reach for the stars and you may hit the moon, reach for the moon and you will probably hit the ground.' Aim high and go for it!

Change: Change is inevitable and not a bad thing. The whole world is changing and evolving every second of every minute. You need to adapt to the changes, even pre-empt the changes or better still be an instigator of 'the wave'. I guarantee that if you do not open yourself up to changes in your world then you will get depressed and stressed. I know this at first hand, I have been there.

The life programme: I have learnt to think of life in relation to IT projects. Life is a programme of change that comprises of many sub-projects within it. Just like IT projects, some miss their milestones and other projects fail but inevitably the programme runs its course and concludes. My recommendation to you is to become the programme manager, to take control of your existence and not to be afraid of all the hard project work that goes into it.

Mistakes and failures: Another reality check, please! We all make mistakes and fail. In IT the term 'GIGO' (garbage in, garbage out) springs to mind. Having read this book you will have realised that I had some emotional garbage early on in life that was 'fed in' and that as a result I also gave a lot of 'garbage out' for a long time (I hope you do not think this book is garbage by the way).

Humans can dream and make decisions. This ability not only differentiates us from other animals but it also makes us fallible. Failure should be seen as an experience and all experiences, whether good or bad, are things that we can learn from. Therefore, in my opinion, *all* experiences are good.

Going down many dead-ends is not failure in my mind; it is part of the course to find your 'Cheese' (read this book if you do not get the last sentence).

Do not trample on people! Getting to the top by standing on someone's head is not the way to do it! If you think you are some sort of 'Gordon Gecko' character from the 1980's film *Wall Street*, please re-think your style. You may get to the top but you will have a few problems once you get there:

+ You will not have any friends
+ You will not be able to trust anyone, and

- You will only remain at the top a short while before some-one else takes you out of the game.

I am a great believer in 'what goes around comes around' and have seen it several times. You should achieve your goals via hard work, commitment and being yourself. People respect managers and directors who are able to demonstrate that they can also do the jobs of their workforce and treat them with respect. Also, achieving things in this way is very personally fulfilling.

Simplicity: This term is the cornerstone of my life now. Indeed not many people know that I have a Tattoo on my left shoulder of a symbol meaning 'simplicity'; this is a constant reminder to me not to overcomplicate my life.

It has taken me a lot of years to come down to this very small word that means so much. Basically, if you over-complicate things they go pear-shaped, be they in life or work.

I have people coming to me all the time with these fantas-tic and well-thought out ideas but they can be very complex. I always take one step back and think how they might be sim-plified. Simplification means that problems then become more manageable. Imagine something as simple as a child's stand-on scooter. The scooter is easy to use: the child picks it up, holds the handle, stands on it with one foot and pushes off with the other. Now let's do the 'human' thing and over-complicate and over-engineer this scooter by adding a motor. By doing this we have just created multiple failure points to keep an eye on and other issues relating to rules, for example age needed to ride it? Can it go on roads? Blah, blah, blah. All the child wanted to do was get from A to B in a fun way! I hope you get my meaning.

Family: Your family should always be your number one priority. Without their love and support there really is no point in being successful. Nearly every senior executive I know has been or is getting divorced as they forgot to pay attention to their family on the way up – myself included. If you genuinely love your family, make sure you bring them into your plans and that they fully understand the implication of what you want to achieve. Riding a roller-coaster is much more fun with other people on the ride too!

Networking: No, not the 'techie' thing. This is about building rapport with like-minded people. Even when writing this book I bounced the idea off members of my network and I do this more and more often in everything I do. However, you must be prepared for the fact that networking is a two-way street and you will also have to provide advice and services 'non-gratis', but it can be very personally fulfilling when you do. I recently looked at how many business cards I had collected over the past 2 years from various events and supplier visits, 200! Just imagine how many of these people could be potential clients or great networking contacts, they will also have networks of people they know so 200 contact could turn into 10+ times 200. Wow!

Communication: It is very important that you communicate with teams of people and individuals working for you and also with stakeholders. Think about it, if you were not given the reason for doing something, would you be willing to do it? You need to tell your teams about your plans and dreams and get their agreement and buy-in. This will make your path much easier and they will join you on what could be a fantastic journey.

Innovation: Fact – if companies do not innovate, they will stagnate. Companies need to innovate and the IT infrastructure needs to be modelled to allow the company to do so. In the fast-moving world of business, changes need to be put into action as soon as possible to allow for market advantage to be achieved.

As the head of the IT 'engine room' you need to establish an environment where innovation is the norm and not the exception. To do this you firstly need to look at what you have and assess its capabilities, not only technological capabilities but also your human capital (people). You then need to think about the application of these capabilities within your company's environment. You may be pleasantly surprised at what can be achieved by adapting and manipulating your existing assets. If you are not, then think of creative ways to change these and ensure they remain flexible in a changing environment.

Professionalism: Being a professional to me means being honest about your own capabilities. You need to make sure that your employer and employees understand what you can and cannot do for them. It also means playing things straight, you try to be whiter than white.

Loyalty: This is a hard one. You should be loyal to the company you work for and not the person you work for or report to. Why? People change and move on; companies hopefully remain. Our contracts both permanent and interim are with a company, a legal entity, not with a person. Therefore we have to do what we feel is right and what we are paid to do for the company. This then enables us to become removed from personal situations if it is for the better good of the company.

Credentials: Integrity in what you do is, I think, important. For example, your résumé should be a complete and truthful representation of your career to date (if not, you will be found out!). This, together with references, provides an employer with a credible view of you. People listen and work with credible, plausible people; they do not work with idiots!

Passion: This is a key quality I always look for in anyone I work with or interview. If someone is passionate about what they do, then I know that they are going to deliver the goods for the company.

If you put someone in front of me who has university degrees that provide credibility but I see no passion, and someone without a degree but who has the passion, the latter will get a shot at it. Why? Because they may turn out to be a star for the company and may even become a life long friend to me.

I have not told you anything here that commonsense does not dictate. These are things that I have realised over the years and now play a part in my life. I hope they help you a little.

End-to-end: It is especially important as a manager or director to be able to view things E2E. This is something I am naturally very good. Sometimes it can be perceived as you being a little negative at times, especially when people are totally focused on the wonderful idea that they have but have not thought it fully through. Having the ability to look at everything in the chain and asses risks, opportunities, impact etc, allows you to very quickly determine if something will work or not. This can save a lot of time and effort spent on the wrong things.

End Game: Do not confuse this with E2E. You must focus on the *end game*, but more than this you must focus your team on the end game. They need to understand what success looks like or how will they or you know when it has been achieved. Therefore if the end point has not been defined in anything you do then it will have a high probability of failure, this is not just in business but also personal life. We all need to feel like we have achieved what we set out to do.

Be yourself: I have learnt over the years that you cannot be something you are not. People either like you or they do not, this is not something you can control or manipulate as it will soon be found out if you try. I am quite an introverted person and have worked hard to push myself into situations and learn from them, this builds character and then feeds into who you are, rather than putting a lot of effort into trying to convince people of something you are not, and failing. The reality is that people buy people, not products or services.

2 MUCH 2 YOUNG

APPENDIX B
POTTED CAREER HISTORY

I HAD TO PUT my full career history to date somewhere in the book and felt that this is as good a place as any so as not to bore you to death. I have already told you about the Youth Opportunities Programme and Apricot, so I will move on to my next position and will try to keep it interesting rather than provide a curriculum vitae. I am not going to use any company names here that have not already been used as I feel it would be unfair on them and I run the risk of getting my legs slapped in some way.

I left Apricot to learn a little about other aspects of the computer industry. The company I moved to was one of the many dealerships for Apricot and other manufacturers selling hardware and software, mainly to smaller companies. They were not a particularly large business and this was something I liked.

My role in the company was to provide technical support before and after sales. One of the main focus areas for me was implementing some of the first local area networks for businesses. Apricot and IBM were some of the first pioneers of LAN technology in this area and I wanted to be involved. I spent hours studying books on LAN protocols such as TCP/IP and the different topologies of networks. However, the greatest thing I got from this position was greater contact with the end users and the public. This meant that I also had to develop some communication skills rather than just using tech-talk.

I left the company after about a year or so. The company gave me a very small pay rise, which I was not very pleased about. I remember telling the MD that I could probably spend it in a lunchtime pub session on a single beer and promptly resigned. Oh, the impetuousness of youth … lol.

Out of work, I made a few calls and got a position back at Apricot in another division of the company; a newly created network support team. The team consisted of four people: two software and two hardware engineers (me being one of the latter). The team was created to go out and trouble-shoot problems that dealers had created with clients, that is, installing things incorrectly, a common occurrence at this time. It was a great feeling being in a new team and with status in the company. I got to see a lot of research and development going on and some of the new software coming on the scene at the time, such as pre-release Microsoft Windows and Novell Netware.

At this time a programme was on the television called 'Trouble-shooter', involving Sir John Harvey-Jones, the late business guru, being invited into troubled companies to offer a strategy for turn-around. As Apricot was struggling with sales due to the success of the IBM PC and it becoming the standard for all personal computers, the CEO of Apricot invited him in. Sounds like a good idea? What a nightmare this turned out to be for the employees.

Basically the advice, to everyone's astonishment, was to pull out of manufacturing and concentrate on service provision. I remember the aftermath well; more than one hundred people in the support division that I worked for were summoned one by one into a small office and made redundant. Apricot was downsizing. I thought I would be okay; part of a new team and at the forefront of technology. I stupidly and naively thought that I had been called into the office to be given my new anticipated company car... doh! ... What a Homer Simpson moment that was.

Lesson learnt, 'Do not think you are indispensable; you are not.'

I sent my CV to all the employment agencies in the area. I also called them many times on the phone to keep my name at the top of the pile.

One agency was very interested in my Local Area Networking experience and asked me if I would consider becoming a lecturer on the subject in their training division. To be honest, I would have considered road sweeping if it could stop me from 'signing on' at the social security offices.

I had an initial interview with the MD of the training division at his home, a very nice house in the countryside. We got on well and he asked me to prepare a fifteen-minute presentation on networking to be presented to his team of lecturers a few days later. You know a lot about me by now; how do you think I felt about presenting? Well, I did not sleep for a few days. There was no such thing as PowerPoint then; my slides were hand-written and copied onto acetate for projection.

I pushed myself hard, did the presentation and got offered the position of lecturer in **networking and communications**. One thing I omitted to say is that I was twenty-two years of age and quite 'wet behind the ears' really.

My first task was to develop a presentation and coursework for the networking and communications course, which would enable the sales representatives to sell the course – with me as lecturer. Talk about bad luck, my first course was to be for a group of scientists at GCHQ, the government so called 'spy centre' in Cheltenham. These guys really knew their stuff. The course was a three-day event. On the first day I did the usual stand in front of the group with a white board and projector trying to teach them about RS232 communications. Stupid really; they already knew this and were bored out of their heads.

I changed my tack the next day and brought in a number of personal computers, a file server, cabling and network software. I positioned everything around the room in pieces and told them to put it together without the aid of manuals, just guidance from me. They loved this and while they were making mistakes and asking questions about components on LAN networking cards and so on, I was giving them advice and tips.

I learnt something valuable on that day; **you should never just plough down a given path if that path is not working. Be prepared to change and adapt and to do it quickly!**

At the time I also delivered application courses in Lotus 1-2-3 spreadsheets, wordcraft & wordstar word-processing and other courses such as the management of IT systems. I grew in stature as a lecturer as my confidence grew. I also taught myself the BASIC programming language and then delivered a course in it to a job training scheme evening class. These were people who had decided to change their present career for one in IT. I felt good.

The training division later got sold off and the previous owners moved me to their software division, feeling that I had a lot more to offer them.

I retrained myself very quickly to be an analyst programmer and learnt COBOL. Once again, I was mostly self-taught. The software house I now worked for wrote and maintained applications for local government authorities in the areas of management of environmental health and public utilities. This work never really grabbed my attention once I had become proficient in the language, things became a little repetitive so I decided to leave; not enough activity to keep my interest, I suppose.

I decided to go back to my hardware maintenance past and work for an electronic point of sales (EPOS) solutions provider. The company provided these solutions to public houses, restaurants and hotels around the UK.

I started as a service engineer, visiting lots of locations and repairing tills and computers, but as usual this was not enough to keep me happy. Within a short period of time I became the senior engineer and a regional office controller for the company. I eventually left this company to work nearer to home and realised that being a 'technician' was not what I really wanted to do with my life.

A few years later I heard that one of the co-directors of the company had crashed his helicopter when taking off. The person in question had created this company with his partner, and made it very successful. It was very sad to hear the news.

I took up a position with a local, small software house. I learnt to program in a language called MUMPS that was DEC equipment based. During this time I helped write and support applications for manufacturing, financial management and stock control, including a revolutionary automated re-ordering system based on stock level historical and predicted usage. This application financially saved the company I wrote it for, as it kept their stockholding down and started to introduce the concept of 'just in time' (JIT) to them.

I really did enjoy my five years with the company. It is just a pity it ended with them firing me (read previous chapters).

I became the senior analyst for a well-known manufacturer of television and video display units. My job was to ensure the systems and services were maintained for the production and office environments. I also designed, but never got to implement, a state of the art high speed LAN for them.

In my first year with the company I carried out a stock audit and found that in previous years they had overstated the stock value by a few million pounds. This meant that the company had no money to invest in new systems for some time to come. The thought of babysitting the existing systems for an undetermined amount of time was too much for me and I decided to take control of my future a bit more. I decided to leave to be a contractor.

C.P.C. stood for Caroline, Phil and Charlotte. This was the name of my new company. To contract I needed to create a company. I was very nervous about taking the leap into contracting, but I learnt quite quickly that the art of contracting is about a number of things:

1. Make sure you can do what you say you can in your CV.
2. Establish good rapport with agencies that can place you with companies.
3. Try to get invoices paid weekly rather than monthly to help improve your cash flow, especially in the early days. Or even have your invoices 'factored'.
4. Hound the agents by telephone and keep them actively trying to place you. You need to work and earn money.

We were financially broke at this time, with a young daughter and Caroline was not working full-time. To fund the creation of the company I sold my only asset, our car, on the premise that I could lease another vehicle through the company I was forming. A bit of a gamble, but it worked out okay.

I had a pet name for my agents; I called them 'pimps' and I was their 'bitch'. I meant this in a nice way, as this is exactly how I see contracting, as a form of prostituting yourself with the agent taking a slice of the pie and hopefully looking after you.

My first contracting assignment was with a global electronics company. I had to design and write a system for the production and management of international shipping documents. This was not a very hard task for me and they decided to retain my service to work through other software glitches on their systems.

At the time they started a project to implement ERP under the guise of SAP R/3 across the company. This was my first exposure to SAP and I was eager to find out more. The company kept me on to help extract and convert the legacy data to the new solution and as I worked I realised that the more interesting thing to do, and which was potentially a larger 'money-spinner' for me, was the project management of such implementations.

After leaving this assignment I found a position as programme office manager for a large food retail company's SAP implementation and business re-engineering programme. Did I have a clue what I was doing when I took the job on? No, but I did know that within only a few days I would have the knowledge needed and that this was an opportunity for me to observe programme and project managers at close range and learn from them.

I got involved in all aspects of the programme and would like to think that I added some real value to the successful outcome of it. I also managed to project manage the implementation of a support structure for the 'go-live' of the process changes and the system and this encouraged me further.

It's worth pointing out here that I consider project management to be about commonsense and managing portions of time effectively. Not to be confused with rocket science - project management is far harder ☺

When you are a contractor you sometimes have to take on work that you would not normally wish to do; beggars can't be choosers and all that. This was the case with my next role. I ended up working in the south west of England for a software company who had developed medical records systems. The Year 2000 was approaching and the majority of the programs written had never catered for anything above the year 1999 and were usually only two digits. My job was to go through suites and suites of programs looking for these dates, making them four digits and ensuring they worked. This was a very tedious task, but it paid well. I also helped manage the full regression testing of the software to ensure it worked.

I am pleased to say that everything worked well. At the end of the project they wanted me to stay on for another assignment, but I decided it was time to progress my project management further. Anyway, travelling four hours each way every week became a bit of a drag.

My next assignment was with a large pharmaceutical company based in the East Midlands. The company had been implementing SAP but the large consulting company involved had left them in the lurch. They had delivered very little in the way of the function required and had not rolled the system out. My job was to pull the project out of the jaws of death. This was a big tester for me and it provided my first real full-on project management job. Worse than this was the fact that I was asked to manage another four projects for different system implementations all at the same time! I rose to the challenge and I like to think that I did a good job as everything was delivered to the deadlines and cost constraints. This also introduced me to more program management techniques and during the assignment I studied and became a qualified PRINCE 2 practitioner.

This was the only company I ever worked for where on occasion I caught a corporate jet to get to work. They were making a lot of money at the time.

As you are aware, I have very little in the way of academic qualifications so I am very proud of the PRINCE 2 qualification I achieved. I not only passed it, but passed at a level that allowed me to teach the subject.

My next role was based in the M4 corridor for a large consulting firm who were looking for a 'stage project manager' on a bid that they were working on for an outsourcing deal with a bank. Well, things got a little interesting when I found out that not only did they want me to manage a stage of the project, but I also had to produce every piece of project documentation for the bid: project plans, work packages, project initiation documents, and so on. I enjoyed getting my teeth into this and I am pleased to say that the bid was successful and I managed the first two stages of the project prior to their own consultants taking over.

In fact, things went so well that they asked me to take on some programme work for another 'outsource' they had. This role had me running all over the country, as the sites were dispersed, but yet again the program was a success and I got a nice reference from them. I worked for the company for three years in all.

I cannot remember ever being part of anything that failed. Probably luck more than judgement I suppose.

During all of this I also realised that I had the potential to source and bring in my own sub-consultants to help on projects. This I did and my company was becoming quite successful until the point when I had to close it during my marital difficulties.

This brings me to my last permanent position, the one at Amtrak, which you know all about.

So that was my resume, interesting? Probably not, I find them boring…lol

INNOVATION AWARD – JUDGES COMMENTS

PRESS RELEASE

AMTRAK'S PHIL YOUNG WINS CIO INNOVATOR OF THE YEAR AWARD

Phil Young, Head of IT operations at Amtrak, has won the prestigious CIO Innovator of the Year Award. The award is given to the Chief Information Officer or IT Director who has demonstrated a willingness to innovate using products or services from growth technology firms in the UK. Young has pioneered the use of the latest web technology and wireless data collection from two UK emerging technology firms.

The winners of the 8th annual UK Technology Innovation & Growth Awards were announced at a spectacular gala evening at the London Metropole. An influential audience of over 600 investors, technology companies, users, and experts gathered to celebrate the individuals and companies that are driving the UK technology industry into the future.

The CIO Innovator of the Year Award recognises individuals who have gone the extra mile to identify the right technologies for their business and been open to taking risks on new and innovative solutions. Young has revolutionised Amtrak's business.

The awards ceremony was hosted by former CNN anchor John Defterios, the evening was opened by Rt Hon Sir Richard Needham, Deputy Chair, Dyson, who emphasized the importance of innovation and entrepreneurial flair to the continuing health and growth of the UK technology sector. Sponsored by PriceWaterhouseCoopers, the awards received a record number of entries and were judged by a panel of experienced industry figures, analysts, journalists and technologists.

The other finalists for the CIO Innovator of the year award were Peter Pedersen of **Blue Square**, Al-Noor Ramji of **BT Group**, JP Rangaswami of **Dresdner Kleinwort Wasserstein** and Frank Coyle of **Menzies Distribution**.

JUDGES COMMENTS

CIO Innovator of the Year

Winner: Phil Young

The judges felt that successful innovation is about doing two things well. Establishing and nurturing the correct environment for innovation to thrive and then ensuring the successful implementation of the project to make the innovation reality. Phil Young at Amtrak demonstrated how he has addressed each of these aspects of innovation successfully and how the result has benefited Amtrak's business. Other case studies (or entries) demonstrated capability in one or other of the skills we were looking for whereas Phil Young stood out as being able to prove the success of both aspects.

2 MUCH 2 YOUNG

APPENDIX D
ABOUT THE AUTHOR

Phil is a senior executive whose career spans a period of over twenty-five years during some of the most exciting times of business and technology development. His career has culminated in him being awarded the 'CIO Innovator for the UK Award' at the Technology & Growth awards.

He currently lives in Worcestershire with his wife and 3 children. After leaving permanent employment in 2007 he started his own company Johnson-Young Associated Limited. Another aspect to his working life is in helping smaller companies overcome growth obstacles or working with start-up companies to develop and deliver strategies for success.

Phil regularly writes articles on various subject matter such as; *Innovation, Why projects need managing and factors in making a small business work.* He regularly takes part in panel and public speaking events.

Phil also spends his spare time working with his wife to develop her own business brand and together they enjoy playing Golf and taking time out for family holidays.

If you would like to contact Phil then please email him at:

contactphil@j-ya.com

He would be delighted to hear from you.

ABOUT THE AUTHOR

www.ingramcontent.com/pod-product-compliance
Lightning Source LLC
Chambersburg PA
CBHW030520100426
42813CB00001B/97

* 9 7 8 1 4 2 5 1 8 4 7 6 6 *